An Introduction to
Marketing
Experimentation

M. VENKATESAN
University of Massachusetts

ROBERT J. HOLLOWAY
University of Minnesota

An Introduction to Marketing Experimentation

METHODS, APPLICATIONS, AND PROBLEMS

THE FREE PRESS, *New York*
COLLIER-MACMILLAN LIMITED, *London*

The Free Press
A Division of The Macmillan Company
866 Third Avenue, New York,
New York 10022

Collier-Macmillan Canada Limited
Toronto, Ontario

Library of Congress Catalog Card Number
71–143510

printing number
1 2 3 4 5 6 7 8 9 10

Figure 5-1 (page 77), Figure 5-2 (page 78),
and Table 5-1 (page 79) courtesy of E.
Wallerstein, president of Communication
and Media Research Services, Inc. Split
Cable patent numbers are: U. S. Patent
Office, patent #3366731, patented 1968;
and Canadian Patent Office, patent
#794974, patented 1968.

ISBN-10: 1-4165-7868-4

ISBN-13: 978-1-4165-7868-0

This book is dedicated
to those who as students, teachers, and practitioners
have furthered the development of the
experimental method in marketing

Contents

PREFACE

1. BASES OF EXPERIMENTATION 1

    WHAT IS AN EXPERIMENT? 1

    TYPES OF EXPERIMENTS 1

    ILLUSTRATIONS OF MARKETING

        EXPERIMENTS 2

        Customary prices 2

    CAUSE AND EFFECT 3

    THE SEARCH FOR CAUSES 3

    PROBLEMS 7

2. INGREDIENTS OF AN EXPERIMENT 11

    PROBLEM STATEMENT 12

    HYPOTHESES 12

    VARIABLES 13

        Types of variables 14

    INTERACTION 15

    PROBLEMS 19

    ADDENDUM TO CHAPTER 2 27

3. INGREDIENTS—DESIGNING AN EXPERIMENT 29

    MEASUREMENT 29

        Verbal measures 30

        Mechanical measuring devices 30

        Direct measures 32

    SUBJECTS 32

    CONTROL OF VARIABLES 33

        What is control? 34

    TECHNIQUES OF CONTROL 34

        Elimination 35

        Constancy of conditions 36

        Balancing 36

        Counterbalancing 37

        Randomization 37

    MANIPULATION 37

    PROBLEMS 39

4. INGREDIENTS—DESIGN ASPECTS 49

    DESIGN ASPECTS 49

    EXPERIMENTAL DESIGNS 49

      Before–after designs 50

      Randomized designs 52

      Latin squares 53

      Carry-over designs 54

      Factorial designs 55

    EXPERIMENTAL PROCEDURE 57

      Conducting an experiment—an illustration 57

    PROBLEMS 63

5. EXPERIMENTS—FROM THE LABORATORY TO THE FIELD 75

    LABORATORY EXPERIMENTATION 75

    FIELD EXPERIMENTS 77

    SIMULATION 79

    PROBLEMS 83

6. ANALYSIS AND PRESENTATION OF RESULTS 89

    FORMAT OF PRESENTATION 91

    ILLUSTRATION OF ANALYSIS AND PRESENTATION OF RESULTS 92

      An experimental study of customer effort, expectation, and satisfaction 93

    PROBLEMS 101

7. APPLICATIONS AND IMPLICATIONS 107

    SOURCES OF EXPERIMENTAL STUDIES 107

    PROBLEMS 111

Appendix A. MECHANICAL MEASURES 121

Appendix B. VALIDITY OF EXPERIMENTS 125

Appendix C. LABORATORY EXPERIMENTS IN MARKETING: THE EXPERIMENTER EFFECT 127

Appendix D. ETHICS IN EXPERIMENTAL RESEARCH 135

REFERENCES 139

Preface

One of the important signs of marketing's maturation as a discipline is the development of its research methodology. A significant first step was taken in the attempt to apply a scientific approach to marketing problems. Marketing research methods have come a long way since the days of the first research efforts.

Traditionally, the physical sciences and the behavioral sciences have made use of experimentation in the laboratory as this methodology provided better control of variables. Researchers in the marketing area are finding it necessary to achieve greater control in their work, and logically they have turned to experimentation—both in the laboratory and in the field. However, experimentation in marketing is still in its infancy, as marketing phenomena are complex and progress in the development of methodology is of necessity rather slow.

The few existing books on the subject of experimentation in marketing have concentrated primarily on the analysis of the experimental data and have emphasized statistical experimental designs. The other aspects of experimentation in marketing—defining variables, formulating control and manipulation techniques, planning and conducting an experiment—have been largely neglected. Yet, both kinds of knowledge are necessary. In psychology and sociology, traditions have been established whereby laboratory manuals aim at providing the important nonstatistical links in experimental procedures. Our aim is to guide students toward developing an appreciation and understanding of laboratory and field experimentation as a methodology, and to help them acquire an ability to plan and execute a variety of marketing experiments. With this in mind, we have tried to provide (1) text material relevant to the topics, (2) illustrations taken from the marketing literature, and (3) problems for the student so that he can apply his knowledge to various marketing experiments. It is hoped that the illustrations will generate the student's interest and curiosity and that the problems will bring about a satisfying sense of involvement. Thus, considerable participation is possible for both the instructor and the student.

Our modest aim is to introduce the student to the experimental methodology and to point out its salient aspects. Therefore, we have deliberately not attempted to include any statistical analysis (processing of experimental data), nor have we included any discussions on the statistical aspects of experimental design. This book is not intended to be a quick review of experimental designs or of statistical inference. Experimental procedure, on the other hand, is discussed in some detail.

An Introduction to Marketing Experimentation is flexible enough in format to be used in a "marketing research" course with selected readings, or it can be used alone, particularly for a separate course in "marketing experimentation." This book has been used at the University of Minnesota in manuscript form and at the University of Massachusetts. The interest generated among students has been encouraging. Several colleagues offered helpful comments and we are grateful to them. We particularly want to acknowledge with thanks the thoughtful comments by Professors Harold H. Kassarjian at UCLA, Richard W. Pollay at the University of Kansas, James R. Taylor at the University of Michigan, John G. Myers at the University of California at Berkeley, and Gerald Albaum at the University of Oregon. Professor C. W. Rudelius at the University of Minnesota contributed some problems in the design section.

Amherst, Mass.   M.V.
Minneapolis, Minn.   R.J.H.

An Introduction to

Marketing
Experimentation

1

Bases of experimentation

If marketing is to become more scientific, more experiments are necessary. The fact that the number of marketing experiments has increased several times over has been one of the encouraging developments in the last five years, although the percentage of all projects done as experiments is still very small.[1]

What is an experiment?

Experiments are *observations*. The way in which observations are made in an experiment differs from other research methods in that the investigator (experimenter) *deliberately intervenes* in the situation. The experimenter has some degree of *control* over the variables and the conditions under which the variables are observed.

The controlled experiment has proven of invaluable assistance in securing information on relationships and particularly on the form of relationships. It provides a means whereby several people can perform the same act and secure the same information. This method can yield very effective information for testing ideas and securing data upon which to base universal agreement.[2]

Spectacular advances in knowledge in the natural sciences have been aided by experimentation. The use of experimentation in the social sciences, however, has not been widespread for a variety of reasons.

We can indicate what happened to sales in a specific situation when advertising was increased, but we have difficulty in providing information about the form of the relationship which prevailed. Changes in sales could have been related to factors in addition to the advertising or completely independent of the advertising. This problem makes it difficult to establish universal agreement on the relationship between advertising and consumer behavior. We begin to make progress when we can at least isolate all factors but the relationship between advertising and consumer behavior.[3]

What experiment can do is to minimize the errors of observation that are inseparable from casual encounters, or at any rate from unplanned ones. The experimenter knows what he is letting himself in for, and is in a position to judge soberly whether (and in what respects) the game was worth the candle. ... Experiment is the device by which we strip appearances from reality, and by putting matters to a test, distinguish dependent from independent variables. And by design, our ingenuity works to maximize the information that can be extracted from recalcitrant data.[4]

Types of experiments[5]

There are different types of experiments. The following classification of experiments designates the many things that experiments can accomplish—it is not intended to be an exhaustive categorization of experiments.

1 *Methodological experiments*

Concerned with refining and improving the techniques employed in experiments.

2 *Pilot studies*

"Trial runs" or "pre-tests" that will play a major part in setting up the major experiments.

1. Reprinted with permission from Harper W. Boyd and Ralph Westfall, *Marketing Research: Text and Cases*, Revised Edition (Homewood, Ill.: Richard D. Irwin, Inc.), 1964, p. 92.

2. Paul H. Rigby, *Conceptual Foundations of Business Research* (New York: John Wiley & Sons, Inc.), 1965, p. 193. Readers are also referred to Green and Frank's definition: "Experiments are studies in which implementation involves intervention by the observer beyond that required for measurement, whereas nonexperimental studies involve only that degree of intervention required for measurement." Paul E. Green and Ronald E. Frank, *A Manager's Guide to Marketing Research* (New York: John Wiley & Sons, Inc.), 1967, p. 69.

3. Rigby, *op. cit.*, p. 193.

4. Abraham Kaplan, *The Conduct of Inquiry* (San Francisco: Chandler Publishing Company), 1964, p. 147.

5. This classification of experiments follows Kaplan's discussion. (*Ibid.*, pp. 148–154.)

3 *Heuristic experiments*

These experiments are designed to "generate ideas, to provide leads for further inquiry or to open up new lines of investigation. . . . A special kind of heuristic experiment may be called *exploratory*."[6]

4 *"Fact-finding" experiments*

Perhaps the most common experiments in scientific context. They are aimed at the determination of relationships between variables in well-defined experiments.

5 *Simulation experiments*

These are experiments on a model. ". . . they are designed to learn what will happen under certain 'real' conditions related in a definite way to the experimental ones."[7]

6 *Theoretical experiments*

"When experiments are explicitly planned and interpreted in the light of comprehensive theories."[8]

7 *Illustrative experiments*

"The classroom repetition of an experiment which is important either historically or in the current state of the discipline is an example of an illustrative experiment, as is any replication undertaken by a scientist in the spirit of wanting to see for himself how it comes out."[9] They also serve to train future researchers.

Even though a number of different types of experiments are indicated in the preceeding classification, *the general experimental method* remains the same, regardless of the type of problem to which it is applied. Strictly speaking, the preceeding classification relates to the different types of problems and to the purposes for which the experimental methodology is used. To clarify this matter, McGuigan contrasts exploratory with confirmatory (fact-finding) experiments:

The type the experimenter uses depends on the state of the knowledge relevant to the problem with which he is dealing. If there is little knowledge about a given problem, the experimenter performs an exploratory experiment. Lacking much knowledge about the problem he is usually not in a position to formulate a possible solution—generally, he cannot postulate an explicit hypothesis which might guide him to predict such and such a happening. He is

simply curious, collects some data, but doesn't really have any basis on which to guess how the experiment will turn out. . . . It can be seen that the exploratory experiment is performed in the earlier stages of the investigation of a problem area. As he gathers data relevant to the problem, the experimenter becomes increasingly capable of formulating hypotheses of a more clear-cut nature—he is able to predict, on the basis of a hypothesis, that such and such an event should occur. At this stage of knowledge development he performs the confirmatory experiment, i.e., he starts with an explicit hypothesis that he wishes to test. On the basis of that hypothesis he is able to predict an outcome of his experiment; he sets up the experiment to determine whether the outcome is, indeed, that predicted by his hypothesis.[10]

Illustrations of marketing experiments

The following marketing experiment, which was conducted over 30 years ago, was an attempt to determine cause and effect between prices and sales. It is used as an illustration of experimentation in marketing because it contains most of the ingredients of an experiment to which readers will be referred in the following chapters.

Customary prices

For many years, retail prices in this country have been quoted at one or two cents below the decimal unit—$.49, $.79, $.98, $1.49, $1.98, tell the tale. Several years ago, one of the large mail-order houses undertook an experiment to discover the significance of these customary prices. If they proved to be of no particular importance, substantial economies in accounting were in the offing. The merchandising executives suspected that the pricing tradition survived because of universal indulgence; they believed that, if attacked, it would soon give up the ghost. But this was only a suspicion; hence, they proceeded cautiously.

Excellent opportunities were afforded to control the experiment. The concern issued annually two large catalogues, in the Spring and in the Fall; also two small ones, known to the trade as flyers, aimed at stimulating trade during the dull months. Its principal competitor followed suit. The test was undertaken one Spring. The total edition of the

6. *Ibid.*, p. 149.　　8. *Ibid.*, p. 152.
7. *Ibid.*, p. 150.　　9. *Ibid.*, p. 153.

10. F. J. McGuigan, *Experimental Psychology: A Methodological Approach*, 2nd ed., © 1968, p. 48. Reprinted by permission of Prentice-Hall, Inc., Englewood Cliffs, New Jersey.

catalogue numbered approximately 6,000,000. Variations in merchandise offered and featured—a recognition of economic and climatic differences—resulted in the production of regional catalogues. However, identity rather than dissimilarity was their outstanding characteristic. A group of representative items was selected and priced in several regional catalogues at: $.50, $.80, $1, $1.50, $2; in the remainder of the edition these identical commodities were presented at customary prices: $.49, $.79, $.98, $1.49, $1.98.

The results of the experiment were as interesting as they were perplexing. For certain items, the change from the customary to the rounded price indicated that sales were halved; for others, no appreciable effect was noticeable; for still others, sales were disproportionately large. Throughout the trial the prices of the leading competitor had, of course, remained unchanged. Detailed records of sales in the preceding and present period by classes and by regions permitted the company to account, with a fair degree of certainty, for all variables influencing demand other than the departure from customary prices. Although considerable effort was devoted to interpreting the results, the data would not lend themselves to generalizations. The vice-president in charge of merchandising ventured the guess that the losses were balanced by the gains. He realized full well that a repetition of the experiment might yield sufficient additional data to permit of more definite conclusions. But when a change of one cent a yard led to a loss of $50,000, the experimental zeal, even of a daring business man, was likely to be held in check. Next time the losses might not be offset. One thing was clear: competition was itself a custom limited by the history of institutions, by the psychology of the competitors. The searcher after profits would continue to pay his respects to both.[11]

The term "experiments" brings to our minds certain stereotypes such as the laboratories used by physicists and chemists or even the rat-mazes used by psychologists. In general, experimental methodology does not always involve the use of special equipment or apparatus. Thus marketing experiments are conducted in the "laboratory" with or without special equipment, such as the eye-pupil measurement device, and the natural setting of the market, such as supermarkets. Simulation experiments are also conducted in marketing. These three types of marketing experiments, namely, *laboratory*, *field*, and *simulation*, are discussed in greater detail in Chapter 5.

See Problems 1–1 and 1–2 at the end of this chapter, pages 7 and 8.

Cause and effect

Why conduct experiments? In seeking an explanation of an event, we consider the event the *effect*, and look for another event by which it can be explained—its *cause*. The main objective of experimentation is to establish "causal" relationships between the variables under consideration.

If a scheme of connections between events has been uncovered such that when one event is made or allowed to occur, another necessarily follows, whereas if the first is not allowed to occur, the second will not happen then the first event will be said to be the cause of the other.[12]

The search for causes

Generally, there are three methods by which the cause-and-effect relationships are established. One is the *principle of concomitant variation*, which states that if variation of the intensity of a factor results in parallel variation of the effect, then this factor is a cause. Suppose a brand manager finds a high correlation between the sales of a certain product and the amounts of appropriations for its advertising. This association may serve as a basis for inferring—*not proving*—a causal relationship.

Another classical method is based on the *method of difference*, which states that, if two sets of circumstances differ in only one factor and the one containing the factor leads to the event and the other does not, this factor can be considered the cause of the event. For example, if batches of rats are fed identical diets under identical conditions except that one batch receives also a certain drug, the fact that the rats in this batch die immediately is evidence supporting the hypothesis that the drug kills rats. But it does not prove it. The result may

---

11. Eli Ginzberg, "Customary Prices," *American Economic Review*, Vol. XXVI, No. 2 (1936), p. 296.

12. E. Bright Wilson, Jr., *An Introduction to Scientific Research* (New York: McGraw-Hill Book Company), copyright 1952, p. 24. Used with permission of McGraw-Hill Book Company.

have been due to chance; perhaps the rats would have died anyway from other causes. The difficulty is connected with the expression "identical circumstances." No two circumstances are ever exactly identical; at the very best they must differ either in time or in place and will in fact differ in a practically infinite number of other respects as well.

The so-called *method of agreement* states that if the circumstances leading up to a given event have in all cases had one factor in common, that factor may be the cause sought. This is especially so if it is the only factor in common.

This principle is very important and is widely used. By itself alone it seldom constitutes valid proof of cause, however, mainly because it is very difficult to be sure that a given factor is really the only one common to a group of circumstances. There is, for example, the story of the scientist who was overliberal in enjoying Scotch and soda at a party. The next morning he felt very poorly; so that night he tried rye and soda, again rather too freely. The following day, he again noted the same distressing symptoms. The third night he switched to bourbon and soda, but the morning after was no more pleasant than the others. Analyzing the evidence, he concluded that thereafter he would omit the soda from his drinks, since it was the common ingredient in the three observed cases.[13]

Illustration: media exposure research

The survey method has taught us a great deal about size and quality of audiences and something about advertising exposures therein. But what we really need to know is what all this means in terms of creating sales by advertising. What we are finding today is that we do not understand this relationship between audience and exposure data and sales, in the sense that by knowing the former we can predict the latter with any workable degree of accuracy.

It is not likely that the survey method alone will ever produce this knowledge. It must come, if at all, from application of experimental techniques, because what we are really seeking is a knowledge of causation. So many advertising dollars spent in such and such a way will produce such and such a sales result. And, in general, the experimental method is a more powerful tool for the analysis of causation than the survey method, because of better control over extraneous variables, to keep them from cluttering up the findings.

A simple illustration is the question of position in a newspaper. Is it better for an ad to be up front, or in the back?

Almost everyone assumes that it is better to be

13. *Ibid.*, pp. 32–33.

up front. Survey data would seem to corroborate that assumption. Here, for example, is the average page readership by women of all pages with general news and advertising, based on the 138 continuing studies of newspaper readership:

First 7 Pages   76.6%
Next 8 Pages   72.3%
Next 8 Pages   69.5%
Last 8 Pages   66.1%

Readership declines as we go from the front to the back of the newspaper. Does this prove that it is better to have your ad in the front? Not necessarily so.

Remember, retailers assume the front is the best. It is likely, therefore, that the bigger and better retailers manage to get their ads up front more often than not. Of all the retail ads, these are likely to be the most interesting: the type that will automatically produce a high readership percentage wherever they may appear.

So it may be that the survey data do no more than prove what we know already—that retailers think the front part of the newspaper is the best part for them. We still don't know whether it really is or not. And this, unfortunately, is rather typical of the uncertainty involved in interpreting most survey data.

Can we do any better with the experimental method? Well, let's see. We ran a coupon-type ad every day for five days—split run between page 2 and the last inside left-hand page of the front section. Same ad in each case, and the same surrounding text. One reader got a paper with the ad in the front, the next reader a paper with an ad in the back. Everything else was precisely the same.

This was an offer of limited appeal, and total return was proportionate thereto, but the net result was an equal number of coupon sales from each ad. No difference whatsoever.

The ad in the back pulled neither more nor less than the ad in front.

| Day | Returns from | |
	Front position	Back position
1	122	105
2	85	70
3	46	53
4	31	47
5	43	52
Total	327	327

Statistically speaking, there is nothing here to negate the hypothesis that front and back positions are of equal advertising value. . . .

But it is intuitively obvious that this experimental

approach is more precise than the survey method. With extraneous variables controlled, we can isolate the net effect of the single variable under study.

But you may object that this is, after all, a relatively trivial inquiry. It may be of some practical utility to know which position of the paper is best for advertising, but no earth-shaking principles are involved therein—no deep illumination of basic advertising laws.

To this I would answer that these simple experiments, which often seem trivial, can lead to some rather far-reaching development of general laws which are quite broad in their application.[14]

See Problems 1–3 through 1–6 at the end of this chapter, pages 9 and 10.

14. Alan S. Donnahoe, "A New Direction for Media Research," (Richmond. Virginia: *Richmond-Times Dispatch*), 1961, pp. 1–3.

Namo   Instructor

Date   Section

Problem 1–1

Refer to "Customary prices" on page 2. Could the survey method have been used to study this kind of problem? Explain.

_____

_____

_____

_____

_____

Problem 1–2

A. Look through your local newspaper for advertisements by the department stores in your area. Limit your ads to those where the indicated price does not exceed $30. Search for these ads for a period of seven days (starting with the Sunday newspaper and ending with the Saturday newspaper). Count and classify these ads in terms of prices indicated, as shown below:

Odd-price ads (19¢, $1.49, $1.77, etc.)		Even-price ads (12¢, 20¢, $1.20, etc.)	
Number of ads	*Per cent total*	*Number of ads*	*Per cent total*

Time Period: Starting date _____   Completion date _____

What can you conclude from the above results you have tabulated?

_____

_____

_____

_____

Is this an experiment? Why or why not? _____

_____

_____

_____

B. For the same time period, observe the number of items indicated with "customary" and "rounded" prices. Limit your search to items priced between 50¢ and $5.00.

Ads with customary prices		Ads with rounded prices	
Number	*Per cent total*	*Number*	*Per cent total*

What conclusions can you draw from the results of your observations?

_____

_____

_____

_____

_____

Name	Instructor
Date	Section

Problem 1-3

What are the three methods of establishing cause and effect?

1. _____

2. _____

3. _____

Problem 1-4

The brand manager for Goodwash detergent noticed, during the summer of 1970, that sales had increased about 40 percent. In checking their marketing program, he also found that they had decreased the price for dealers from 57¢ to 49¢ for a box containing 2½ pounds of detergent. Did the price decrease cause the increase in sales? Explain.

_____

_____

_____

_____

_____

Problem 1-5

Refer to "Customary prices" on page 2. For this illustration what appears to be the cause and effects?

Cause _____

Effects _____

Problem 1-6

Shopping cart displays soar sales

To develop a display plan specifically for small items that grocers could arrange with a minimum of effort, the Progressive Grocer recently sparked three series of store tests through the cooperation of self-service operators in Springfield (Mass.) and West Haven (Conn.)....

Nub of the plan was dumping each of the 28 tested items (that ranged from popping corn and pickles to scouring pads and shoe polish) into the top basket of shopping carts and affixing to each a simple hand-printed sign that told a quick story and highlighted the price. Examples: a pie mix display asked "How about a good home made pie tonight? 17¢"; a cart full of pot cleaners boasted "I'll clean your pots 'n pans without an ouch—10c each, 3 for 25c"; and a cheese assortment chortled "They're delicious—try all three—Very Sharp, Smoky, Cheese and Bacon—27¢".

These carts, placed strategically alongside island mass displays, upped sales seldom less than 250% and in some cases 25 times normal movement. And when posed against the well established statistic that a typical mass display will boost sales 100–200% above normal, the average cart display increase of 555% was indeed phenomenal.

In each store, normal movement of the 28 items was watched the week before as well as during the test period. Popping corn jumped from 11 cans to 363 when featured in a cart. After-dinner mints went from 56 to 159 bags, tooth paste from 15 to 90 tubes, facial soap from 28 to 926 bars, and scouring pads from 36 to 139. Shoe polish leaped from 19 to 118 cans, fruit gelatine from 166 to 662 boxes, and mustard from 23 to 118 jars during the week of the display cart test.*

Can you conclude that there is a cause-and-effect relation in the shopping cart study? Explain.

_____

_____

_____

_____

_____

*"Shopping Cart Displays Soar Sales," _Tide_ (March 3, 1950), pp. 37-38.

2

Ingredients of an experiment

Generally, there are several components for any research method. Likewise, there are phases or parts to an experiment. The steps or parts of an experiment are diagrammatically represented in Figure 2-1.

In this chapter, we look at the essential first steps of any experiment, namely, *stating the problem clearly*, *formulating relevant hypotheses for testing*, and *defining the variables* whose relationships are under investigation.

In the next chapter we deal with planning the design of an experiment, particularly the problems of measurement, control and manipulation of variables, and the require-

ments for conducting an experiment, that is, subjects, instructions, and similar important aspects of an experiment.

In Chapter 4, we provide a description of the design aspects of an experiment. An experimental design is mainly concerned with identifying the sources of all variation in an experiment. Our interest in the experimental design is primarily from the viewpoint of using it in setting up an experiment and in planning the experiment. Having developed the entire plan for the experiment, the next step of course is to conduct the study.

An example of an experiment is provided

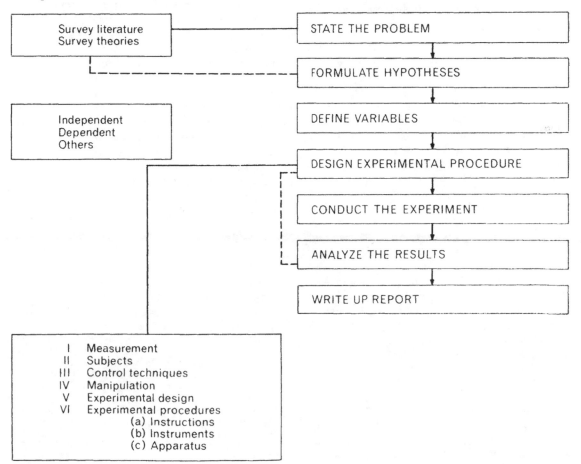

Figure 2-1. *Diagram of an experiment.*

in Chapter 4 to illustrate the mechanics involved in the conduct of an experiment.

In the next step, the experimenter analyzes the data obtained from the experiment. (This is discussed briefly in Chapter 6.) No amount of reading can substitute for the actual practice of conducting an experiment and analyzing the data. Chapter 6 also points out the functions of analysis and provides a commonly used format to report the findings of experimental studies.

The student is strongly urged to familiarize himself with the steps of an experiment before proceeding with the details of the components.

Problem statement

There is a well-known saying that a problem well-stated is half solved. The experimental method, perhaps even more than other research methods, demands a clear definition of the problem since the successful design of the entire experiment depends upon a satisfactory problem statement.

It is not always possible for a researcher to formulate his problem simply, clearly, and completely. He may often have only a rather general, diffuse, even confused notion of the problem. This is in the nature of the complexity of scientific research. It may even take an investigator years of exploration, thought, and research before he can clearly say what questions he has been seeking answers to. Nevertheless, adequate statement of the research problem is one of the most important parts of research. That it may be difficult or impossible to state a research problem satisfactorily at this time should not allow us to lose sight of the ultimate desirability and necessity of doing so. Nor should the difficulty be used as a rationalization to avoid stating the problem. ...

A *problem*, then, is an interrogative sentence or statement that asks: What relation exists between two or more variables? The answer to this question is what is being sought in the research. If the problem is a scientific one, it will always contain two or more variables.[1]

ILLUSTRATIONS

Sales effects of two campaign themes
The purpose of this study was to evaluate the sales effectiveness of a specific promotional campaign.

The objectives of the study were to determine:

1. The over-all sales effectiveness of the promotional program relative to no promotion.
2. The relative sales effectiveness of the two promotional themes.
3. The short-time residual or carry-over effects, if any, of each theme.
4. The effects of the promotional activities for Washington apples on sales of apples from competing areas, and other selected fruits.
5. The influence on sales of apples and other fruits of various merchandizing and advertising practices (e.g., price cuts, display space and newspaper advertising) employed by stores to promote apples and other selected fruits.[2]

An experimental study of the effects of information on consumer product evaluations
The primary purpose of this study was to explore the relationships among the effects of two communication factors and consumer predispositions in a decision-making situation. Communications from two consumer information sources—a product rating publication (*Consumer Reports*) and a salesman—incorporated the environmental cues expected to influence the decision process. Brand preferences and difficulty of product judgment were considered as predispositions which might modify the effects of the communication on the decision process. *The basic objective of the research design was to determine the relative influence of these variables upon product evaluations under controlled conditions.* (Italics are by the authors.)[3]

See Problems 2–1 and 2–2 at the end of this chapter, page 19.

Hypotheses

A *hypothesis* is a conjectural statement of the relation between two or more variables. Hypotheses are always in declarative sentence form, and they relate, either generally or specifically, variables to variables. There are two criteria for "good" hypo-

1. Fred N. Kerlinger, *Foundations of Behavioral Research* (New York: Holt, Rinehart and Winston, Inc.), 1966, pp. 18–19.

2. Peter L. Henderson, James F. Hind, and Sidney E. Brown, "Sales Effects of Two Campaign Themes," *Journal of Advertising Research*, Vol. 1, No. 6 (December, 1961), pp. 2–11.

3. Donald J. Hempel, "An Experimental Study of the Effects of Information on Consumer Product Evaluations," in Raymond M. Haas (editor), *Science, Technology, and Marketing*. Proceedings of the 1966 Fall Conference. (Chicago, Ill.: American Marketing Association), 1966, p. 590.

theses and hypothesis statements. They are the same as two of those for problems and problem statements. One, hypotheses are statements about the relations between variables. Two, hypotheses carry clear implications for testing the stated relations. These criteria mean, then, that hypothesis statements contain two or more variables that are measurable or potentially measurable and that they specify how the variables are related.[4]

The term "hypothesis" is used to indicate that a statement of relationship is considered to be tentative and one to be tested and proven. It really refers to an attitude toward or the status of a statement. This means that any statement, new or old, can become a hypothesis.[5]

ILLUSTRATIONS

Supermarket shelf-space study

There has been a general assumption in the supermarket industry that additional shelf space given to a grocery product would increase the sale of that product. If this assumption were valid, then it would follow that different products should respond in diverse patterns to changes in the amount of shelf space given to them. The purpose of this study, therefore, has been to gain some insight into the relationship between shelf space and sales of different grocery products in supermarkets.

The following hypotheses, based on the above assumptions, have been formulated and tested in this study:

1. Additional shelf space given to a grocery product will increase the sale of the product.
2. The sales of different grocery-product commodities respond in different patterns to changes in shelf space.[6]

An experimental study of customer effort, expectation, and satisfaction

Knowledge about the effects of customer effort and expectation on satisfaction is important to market researchers. To test the effects of effort and expectation on satisfaction, Cardozo formulated the following hypotheses:

1. When customers expend little effort to obtain a product, those who receive a product less

valuable than they expected will rate that product lower than will those who expected to receive, and do receive, the same product.
2. As effort expended increases, this effect decreases.
3. When customers obtain a product less valuable than they expected, those who expended high effort to obtain the product will rate it higher than will those who expended little effort.
4. When customers obtain a product about as valuable as they expected, those who expended high effort to obtain the product will rate it higher than will those who expended little effort.[7]

See Problems 2–3, 2–4, and 2–5 at the end of this chapter, pages 21 and 22.

Variables

In designing an experiment, one must clearly understand and specify the independent variables and all other variables that need to be controlled. First, what is meant by a *variable*?

Variable

Essentially, a variable is anything that changes in value. It is a quality that can exhibit differences in value, usually in magnitude or strength. Thus, it may be said that a variable generally is anything that may assume different numerical values.[8]

A variable is just a symbol, such as X, and numerical values can be assigned to this symbol. For example, let us say we are interested in finding the attitude toward products "Made in Japan." The attitude is the variable. It can vary—it could be favorable, unfavorable, or indifferent, for example. If we designate the symbol X to denote this variable attitude, then the variable X can take on only three values: favorable, unfavorable, or indifferent. A variable X, however, may have two values or a set of values. Some examples of two-valued variables are as follows: male-

4. Kerlinger, *op. cit.*, p. 20.
5. Paul H. Rigby, *Conceptual Foundations of Business Research* (New York: John Wiley & Sons, Inc.), 1965, p. 26.
6. Keith K. Cox, *The Relationship Between Shelf Space and Product Sales in Supermarkets* (Austin, Texas: Bureau of Business Research, The University of Texas), 1964, p. 8.

7. Richard N. Cardozo, "An Experimental Study of Customer Effort, Expectation, and Satisfaction." Reprinted from *Journal of Marketing Research*, Vol. II (August, 1965), p. 245; published by the American Marketing Association.
8. F. J. McGuigan, *Experimental Psychology: A Methodological Approach*, 2nd ed. (Englewood Cliffs, N.J.: Prentice-Hall, Inc.), 1968, p. 5.

female; Republican–Democrat; owns Mustang–Does not own Mustang; buyer–nonbuyer; exposed to advertising appeal–not exposed to advertising appeal. As an example of *X*, the variable taking on a set of values, suppose we are interested in ascertaining the preference for a particular flavor of coffee. Let us assume that each individual is asked to check one of the appropriate numbers below to indicate his preference of the flavor.

Like the flavor — — — — — Dislike the flavor
(1) (2) (3) (4) (5)

The variable is flavor (*X*). The set of values it can take ranges from 1 to 5. Such reasoning can be extended to any variable taking any set of values.

TYPES OF VARIABLES

The most important and useful way to categorize variables is as independent and dependent. This categorization is common to science and to mathematics . . . An *independent variable* is the *presumed* cause of the *dependent variable*, the *presumed* effect. The independent variable is the antecedent; the dependent variable is the consequent. Whenever we say "If *A*, then *B*," whenever we have an implication, *A* implies *B*, we have an independent variable (*A*) and a dependent variable (*B*).[9]

In an experiment, however, the experimenter has control over certain variables. These variables are called the independent variables. Independent variables are variables which the experimenter himself manipulates or changes. As the independent variables are changed, the experimenter observes other variables to see whether they are related to the changes introduced. These variables are called the dependent variables. The problem of the experiment is to determine the relationship between the independent and dependent variables.[10]

A proper design of an experiment involves the identification not only of independent and dependent variables, but also of all the other variables that must be controlled. The reason is that these variables (factors), called *extraneous variables*, are likely to

9. Kerlinger, *op. cit.*, p. 39.
10. Allen L. Edwards, "Experiments: Their Planning and Execution," in Gardner Lindzey (editor), *Handbook of Social Psychology*, Vol. I. (Reading, Mass.: Addison-Wesley Publishing Company), 1954, p. 261.

affect the responses (effects) unless they are controlled or eliminated. An illustration will make this point clear. Suppose a television commercial for brand *Z* gasoline shows two automobiles on a highway. The announcer states that one car has used brand *Z* *without* the special additive and the other has used brand *Z* *with* the special additive. The car without the special additive comes to a stop first, and the car with special additive comes to a stop 10 to 15 yards beyond it. We will assume that both cars used the same quantity of gasoline. The implication of this commercial is that the special additive (the independent variable) results in the extra mileage (dependent variable) of travel. As an experimenter concerned with extraneous variables that could affect the results, we can raise the following questions:

1. Engine: Were the engines of the same size, type?
   Were the conditions of the engines the same (tuning, etc.)?
2. Car: Were the cars of the same condition (gear ratios, carburetor setting, weight, wear and tear, etc.)?
3. Driver: Were the drivers different types?
   Were there differences in acceleration?
   Were there differences in the drivers' weights?

As these questions illustrate, extraneous variables can directly affect results. Similarly, extraneous variables are present in all experiments; these variables must be controlled if the results are to be unequivocal.

Not all extraneous variables are controllable, however. In the above illustration two uncontrollable extraneous variables might be wind drag and the condition of the road. Some extraneous variables, which are very likely to affect the results of marketing experiments and over which the experimenter has little or no control, are the following: weather, competitive efforts (competitive price changes, advertising, and changes in the allocations of salesmen), and business conditions (local, regional, and national).

ILLUSTRATIONS

The influence of in-store advertising

The importance of recency of advertising exposure was supported in an experiment designed to measure the sales effectiveness of Metromedia's fledgling advertising medium which consists of 36-inch, three-dimensional displays in supermarkets. The displays hang from the ceiling so that they are a little above eye level.

Sales and share of market for important national or regional brands of gelatin, coffee, bathroom tissue, and beer were measured for one month in Sacramento, California, by audits in 10 stores in which the brands and leading competitors were advertised in the new medium. The results were compared with the sales and share of market figures for the same brands in 10 control stores which did not have the in-store advertising displays.

The experiment showed striking sales effectiveness for the in-store displays. The test brand of coffee, Hills Bros., had a gain in share of market of 125 per cent in the test stores compared with 10 per cent gain in the control stores. The sales of competing brands declined during the test. Folger's coffee was off 24 per cent in the test stores but gained 4 per cent in the control stores; MJB coffee was off 43 per cent in the test stores and off 28 per cent in the control stores; and Maxwell House was off 9 per cent in the test stores but gained 13 per cent in the control stores.[11]

(In this illustration the *independent variable* was the *in-store displays*, and the *dependent variables* were the *sales* and *share of market* of the brands of product in the experiment.)

An experimental study of the effects of information on consumer product evaluations[12]

In the illustration on page 11, you will recall that the experiment was designed to determine the influence of communications from two consumer information sources—*Consumer Reports* and a salesman's communication—on product evaluations. Product evaluations were obtained after exposing the consumers taking part in the study to the communications.

11. Mary L. McKenna, "The Influence of In-Store Advertising," in J. Newman (editor), *On Knowing the Consumer* (New York: John Wiley & Sons), 1966, p. 114.

12. Hempel, *op. cit.*, p. 590.

The *independent* variable in this situation was *communications from the two sources* and the *dependent* variable was the *product evaluations* obtained from the consumers.

See Problems 2–6, 2–7, 2–8, and 2–9 at the end of this chapter, pages 23 and 24.

Interaction

Marketing experiments do not always involve a single independent variable or a single dependent variable. In many experimental situations, it is interesting to observe the effects of two or more independent variables. In "real life" marketing, there is almost always more than one variable in operation; for example, consider the various elements of the marketing mix—product, price, promotion. Thus, marketing experiments with more than one independent variable are not uncommon. Suppose we are interested in the effects of two marketing variables: price and advertising. It is obvious that price alone as an independent variable may produce certain effects; advertising, treated as an independent variable may also produce some definite effects. In addition, the combination of price and advertising (two independent variables in this case) may produce certain results because of their interaction. Generally, since it is likely that some interaction occurs when two or more independent variables are used, dependent variable or effects may be affected by such interaction. No longer is it a simple relationship between price and sales or between advertising and sales; the results may reflect the interaction of these two variables. The following illustration demonstrates this process of interaction.

ILLUSTRATION

Consider interaction in a marketing context. Suppose you are concerned about the effect on sales of a change in shelf height. You conclude from your study that eye-level shelving is preferable for your product. Let us assume the results were as follows:

Eye level sales: $80
Knee level sales: $40

You are also concerned about the *width* given to the product. Your studies show that the wider shelf spacing is preferable. The results were as follows:

Narrow width sales: $35
Wide width sales: $50

Assume that a series of experiments were conducted involving both the variables— height and width of shelf spacing, as shown below:

Height: Knee level, eye level
Width: Narrow, wide

Width	Height	
	Eye level	Knee level
Narrow	Sales # 1	Sales # 2
Wide	Sales # 3	Sales # 4

Now let us look at some hypothetical results of these experiments to illustrate what we mean by interaction between width and height, the two independent variables. Hypothetical results A and B indicate no significant interaction.

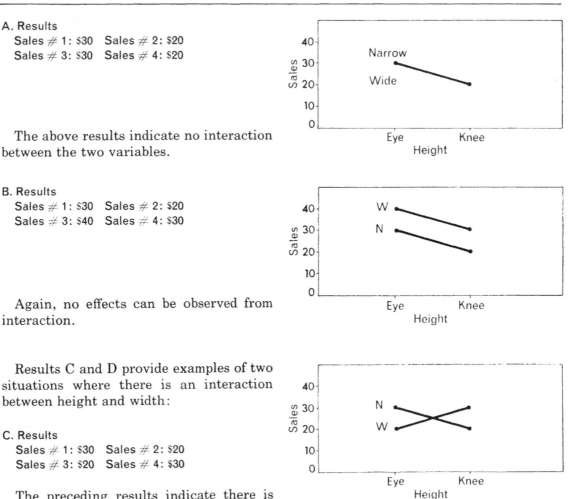

A. Results
    Sales # 1: $30   Sales # 2: $20
    Sales # 3: $30   Sales # 4: $20

The above results indicate no interaction between the two variables.

B. Results
    Sales # 1: $30   Sales # 2: $20
    Sales # 3: $40   Sales # 4: $30

Again, no effects can be observed from interaction.

Results C and D provide examples of two situations where there is an interaction between height and width:

C. Results
    Sales # 1: $30   Sales # 2: $20
    Sales # 3: $20   Sales # 4: $30

The preceding results indicate there is interaction between shelf height and width.

D. Results
  Sales # 1: $30   Sales # 2: $20
  Sales # 3: $20   Sales # 4: $20

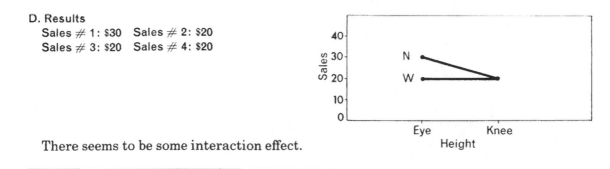

There seems to be some interaction effect.

In the preceding illustrations, it was fairly easy to see the interaction between the two variables and their effects on the dependent variable (sales). However, interaction is not always easy to interpret; and when more than two variables are used, the problem is further compounded. Suppose, in the above example, that color of package, depth of shelf, and location of shelf were used. Then consider day of week, size of supermarket, brands, and so on. Obviously, the experimenter must keep many factors constant while varying one or two in attempting to determine the patterns of interactions.

Interaction results from blending two or more variables. The process of interaction is not the same as blending paint colors, however; the blending of two factors of human behavior is not as predictable as blending red and yellow paint. Thus, in planning for experiments, it is important to have a good understanding of the concept of interactions. One cannot wait until after the results are obtained to analyze whether there was any interaction. Analysis may not be possible unless it has been planned. In the planning stages, one must not only identify the variables involved, but also be aware of a possible interaction between the variables. The experiment must be designed to determine the nature and extent of interaction between the variables. There are special statistical tools (such as factorial designs; see page 55) used in designing experiments that recognize problems of interaction.

See Problems 2–10 and 2–11 on pages 25 and 26.

Name   Instructor

Date   Section

Problem 2-1

Refer to the Ginzberg "Customary prices" experiment (see page 2). State the problem that was investigated in this study.

_____

_____

_____

_____

_____

_____

_____

_____

_____

_____

Problem 2-2

In one experiment, the investigator prepared two advertising appeals for a hi-fi manufacturer. Appeal A showed this product in a party setting (called the "social support appeal" by the investigator) and appeal B gave all the technical information relating to this product (this ad was called the "rational appeal").

What problem do you think the experiment was trying to investigate?

_____

_____

_____

_____

_____

Name	Instructor
Date	Section

Problem 2-3

One experiment involved the use of groups of beer drinkers who tasted (drank) and then rated beer. First they were given beer in nude (unidentified) bottles. After tasting beer from nude bottles, they were given beer from labeled bottles.

What was the principal hypothesis for testing in this experiment?

_____

_____

_____

Problem 2-4

In studies conducted by the Schwerin Research Corporation for the Good Housekeeping Magazine and Institute, it was found that the Good Housekeeping Seal increased the effectiveness of television commercials. The results showed that the seal increased believability as well as the sales effectiveness of the television commercial.

If the seal has such an effect on television commercials, what effect does it have on magazine advertisements? In order to deal with this in an experiment, the following questions are raised: (A) What effect would the seal have on the sales of a product? (B) Is the impact of the Good Housekeeping Seal strong enough to produce a preference switching from a product without the Good Housekeeping Seal to a product with the seal?

How would you state the hypotheses for the Good Housekeeping Seal problem?

Hypothesis A: _____

_____

_____

Hypothesis B: _____

_____

_____

Problem 2-5

Market tests and follow-up revealed that a variety of appeals, such as sociability, pride of ownership, relief from allergies, convenience, less dusting, could be used in the advertising campaign for an electronic air cleaner. From the motives uncovered during the depth interview, the following two stood out: (1) allergy removal and (2) less dusting. These two motives have been transformed into appeals and embodied in the advertisements. Ad A, the allergy appeal advertisement, appeals to the desire for health protection of the individual and the family; ad B stresses the removal of dust predominantly, with a secondary emphasis on removal of pollen content from the air.

The problem is to test the effectiveness of the allergy appeal versus the dust appeal. The criteria on which the appeals are to be measured will be the amount of recall.

Formulate any hypotheses for testing.

_____

_____

_____

_____

_____

_____

_____

_____

_____

Name	Instructor
Date	Section

Problem 2–6

A retail hardware chain is considering a self-service system for its 326 stores. Ten stores have been selected for a trial period of three months. Ten other stores, matching the experimental stores as closely as possible, have been selected as a control group in which the traditional clerk system will operate. Dollar sales for each of the twenty stores will be recorded weekly for the three-month period. Prior to the study, weekly sales will be recorded for a month, a "before" measure. The difference in sales between the experimental and control groups is expected to help the management in its decision.

Identify the independent and dependent variables involved in this study.

Independent variable: _____

Dependent variable: _____

Are there any extraneous variables of which the experiment should be aware?

_____

_____

Problem 2–7

In a study dealing with how an advertisement's size affects responses to it, attention was focused on the following question: What are the effects of large and small advertisements on the eye-movement patterns of a respondent? Are the characteristic eye-movement patterns of an individual modified by the size of the advertisement? Filmed eye movements using an "eye-camera" showed that the size of the ad had little effect.

Identify the variables in this experiment: _____

_____

_____

Problem 2-8

Housewives, Stokely found, feel that green peas belong in a green package, yellow corn in a yellow package, red beets in red—what else? So Stokely changed its old white label to suit. Next week it is launching an ad campaign in newspapers, and later in national magazines, to promote its repackaged line.

The project started six years ago when H. R. Warren, Jr., sales vice president, set out to improve the label. The company, with sales over $200-million, counts its Stokely brand the No. 3 in the country, after Del Monte and Libby's.

Ad agency Lennen & Newell undertook the task. Tests showed that the white Stokely label could be confused with competing brands.

When art experts disagreed over the best background colors, the agency put the question to the women themselves. They asked housewives, in batches of 200—and as many as 1,000 for some products —to match the label pictures of the products and the background color they preferred. Over and over they voted: The background should match the product color. For white vegetables, they chose blue; Stokely didn't give them a choice of white.

Market tests proved the women meant it. In the final test, Stokely sales climbed 44%. In fact, say Stokely officials, wherever the new cans were placed, sales of the entire canned vegetable department jumped too, competing brands and all.*

Identify the independent and dependent variables in the Stokely Study.

_____

_____

_____

Problem 2-9

In one study, conducted in Philadelphia and in Cleveland, oranges with and without color added were displayed side by side in selected supermarket outlets. During the test period, sales were observed for both types of oranges. The size and location of test displays were held constant.

Identify the variables: _____

_____

_____

_____

*"Stokely repackages its canned goods line to match background with product color," *Business Week* (January 25, 1964), p. 48. Special permission granted by *Business Week.*

Name   Instructor

Date   Section

Problem 2–10

Assume that the following results are obtained from a series of experiments involving both height and width of shelf spacing: height—eye level and knee level; width—narrow and wide. Indicate whether there was any interaction by plotting the results in the accompanying diagrams.

		Height	
		Knee level	Eye level
Width {	Narrow	1	2
	Wide	3	4

Experiment I

   1: $30   2: $30
   3: $20   4: $20

   Interaction: _____

Experiment II

   1: $30   2: $30
   3: $30   4: $30

   Interaction: _____

Experiment III

   1: $30   2: $20
   3: $20   4: $30

   Interaction: _____

Problem 2–11

State which of the following questions may be tested experimentally and which may not. Where a test is possible, briefly suggest a method of attack. Where a test is not possible, explain why.

1. Do children from upper classes drink more carbonated beverages than those from lower classes?

2. Is the Mustang (automobile) superior in performance to the Comet?

3. Does the average male today use cosmetics?

4. Is the standard of living higher today that it was ten years ago?

5. Will Shell gasoline with Platformate provide better mileage than Shell gasoline without Platformate?

6. Why do fashions in clothing change?

7. Do low-income consumers have more realistic levels of aspiration than those with higher incomes?

Addendum to Chapter 2

The following listing provides examples of variables that were investigated as independent variables and the types of effects that were observed as dependent variables in experimental situations.

Independent variables

The aspect of the problem or environment which is being studied is, of course, the independent variable. The purpose of this section is to list some of the independent variables in marketing that have been investigated through the experimental method.

Commitment to a decision
Design of a label

Size of display
Display location
Carton with and without picture
Ease of depressing gas pedal
Amount of color
Type of store
Effect of Negro in ad
Width of merchandise line
Location of store
Brand identification
Number of items to carry in inventory
Familiarization
Amount of time to make decision
Imperfect alternatives in choice
Anticipated dissonance
Kind of information available
Amount of effort in buying
Order of presentation
Number items to carry in inventory
Effect of branded merchandise
Type and size of package

Collection of letters, type of
Spot versus network advertising
Amount of blank space in ads
Size of an ad
Advertising television shows
Point of sales promotion

Amount of shelf space
Equipment in store
Bulk packaging
Inducement to buy
Amount of information
Cognitive overlap
Expectation with purchase
Flavor of product
Cues for buying
Group influences
Effect of a warning
Effect of subliminal persuasion
Magnitude of gain: Probability of gain
Interviewer bias
Coder biases
Day versus night television
Frequency of advertising
Amount of promotional expenditures
Ad recognition
Degree of ethics
Ad section
Method of selecting products

Increasing mail response
Effectiveness of salesmen
Quality of sales presentation
Position of the ad
Source effect

Window trim

Dependent variables

The dependent variables show the resultant change in behavior as a result of the experiment or manipulations of the independent variable. Some of the dependent measures used in the experiments reviewed are as follows:

Recall of ad
Sales
Estimate of magnitude
Choice of product
Amount of regret

Changes in attitude
Degree of confidence
Exposure to information
Amount of pupil dilation
Changes in standards
Tabulation of coders

Amount of bad debts collected
Filmed eye movements
Ranking of preferences
Profits
Semantic differential
Choice of store
Magnitude of dissonance reduction

Various kinds of scales
Degree of satisfaction
Ability to identify
Decision to repurchase
Brand choice
Change in awareness of product attributes
Rating of salesmen

Frequently, the experiments utilized several dependent measures. The researchers may have been measuring different effects or they may have had different ways of measuring the same effects. In the field, as in a store experiment, the measure was often the amount of sales. Sales or profits is the ultimate measure of success but much worthwhile marketing experimentation will not be so directly measured.*

*Robert J. Holloway, "Experimental Work in Marketing: Current Research and New Developments," in Frank M. Bass, Charles W. King, and Edgar A. Pessemier (editors), *Applications of the Sciences in Marketing Management* (New York: John Wiley & Sons), 1968, pp. 383–430.

3

Ingredients—designing an experiment

A marketing experiment starts with the statement of the problem and is followed by a formulation of relevant hypotheses and an identification of the variables involved. In order to conduct an experiment to test the formulated hypotheses, a design for the research must be planned. Designing an experiment is very similar to designing a product in that an experiment has to be planned skillfully long before the experiment is actually conducted. Planning the details of an experiment is one of the most important links in the research chain.

In designing an experiment, several important components must be defined carefully, and many times they must be "pretested" before the experiment is ready . At the planning stage, the experimenter must be aware of many problems, such as: How can he measure the effects? How can he manipulate the independent variables? What extraneous variables are likely to affect the relationship under study and what control techniques must be employed? What instructions must be given? What apparatus is needed for conducting the experiment? All these questions point to planning and designing carefully the experimental procedures and techniques. Many times an experimenter overlooks some important point until it is too late. Such lack of planning results in obtaining information that may not be useful and that results in failure to establish a cause-and-effect relationship. Therefore, it is suggested that a series of steps be followed in designing an experiment.

In this chapter the following will be developed: (1) problems of measurement of variables, (2) types of subjects used in marketing experiments, and (3) control and manipulation of variables.

Measurement[1]

In marketing experimentation, we are interested in consumers' reactions to packaging design, color of products, usage, taste preferences, choice of advertising appeals, and the like. In general, our interest is focused on a better understanding of the processes of consumer behavior, the variables that affect this behavior, and the relationships of these variables. Marketing experiments are confined not only to ascertaining the actions and reactions of consumers but also to investigating the physical movement of goods or sales in stores and to determining consumer responses to such variables as price, promotional displays, packaging, and shelf space.

Earlier in the discussion on cause and effect (see page 3) it was pointed out that the main objective of an experiment was to ascertain the causal relationship between the variables under study. Any determination of the relationship between variables is based on a measurement of the effects. In experiments in the physical sciences and in psychology, various extensive and elaborate apparatus are used to measure the effects of variables. Contrary to the popular myth, the mark of a good scientific experiment is not the apparatus requirements. Though some types of apparatus are not uncommon in some marketing experiments (see Appendix A), most of the measures of relationships (effects) are obtained from such simple measures as sales (in dollars or in movement of physical units), choices or preferences

1. This section is concerned only with the operational problems of measurement. Students are urged to familiarize themselves with the concepts of measurement, levels of measurement, and scaling. Discussion of these topics can be found in marketing research textbooks.

indicated by consumers, and in general through paper-and-pencil tests.

Measurement does not have to be complex to be reliable and useful. For example, total sales per day in a store can be measured by totaling receipts of each day; total personnel can be determined by counting the number of people who received a pay check during the week; and total traffic through an airport can be measured by counting the arrivals and departures. However, it is not always as easy to measure as these illustrations would lead one to believe.

Generally, the operational measures used can be classified into three main categories: (1) verbal measures—spoken and written responses, including scaling, paper-and-pencil tests; (2) mechanical measures, such as the measurement of eye movements of advertising readership, pupil dilation measures, and the like (see Appendix A); and (3) direct measures, such as the dollar amount of sales, the amount of profit, and so on. The following illustrations provide a clearer understanding of these three types of measures used in marketing experiments.

VERBAL MEASURES

Illustrations

Experimental study of consumer behavior conformity and independence

The two main objectives of this study were: (1) to gain insight into this phenomenon—conformity to group pressure in the consumer decision-making process; and (2) to study the effects of choice restriction by group pressure in the consumer decision-making process. . . .

The task required the subjects to evaluate and choose the best suit among three identical men's suits labeled A, B, and C. . . .

Three experimental conditions were created for the experiment: Condition I was a Control Condition; in Conditions II and III . . . group pressure (independent variable) was manipulated. . . .

In Conditions II and III the suits were evaluated and the choices were made in a face-to-face group consisting of four individuals, three confederates of the experimenter, and one subject. The confederates had been told to choose B as the *best* suit. In addition, the confederates had been instructed earlier about seating arrangements. In

these two conditions, after the subjects were seated around a table, the experimenter read instructions explaining the task. They were told that after they each examined the suits, they were to publicly announce their choices of the best suit. After examination of the suits, the subjects returned to their seats. Then the experimenter asked each person to announce his choice. Because of the seating and the prior instructions to the confederates, the first confederate was the first to be asked and to respond; then it was the turn of the second and the third confederates respectively. The naive subject was always last to respond. . . . The situation permitted a quantitative measure of yielding . . . and the proportion of choices for A or C was taken to be the measure of nonyielding. The experimenter casually recorded the choices while the subjects were filling out a questionnaire in Phase II. The responses had not been recorded during the public announcements of the choices to avoid creating suspicion about the sequence used in the interrogation.[2]

Deceptive packaging: are the deceivers being deceived?

Naylor, in investigating reactions to deceptive packaging by consumers, used a questionnaire with his subjects to obtain preference information as a function of perceived deception.   (See Figure 3-1.)

MECHANICAL MEASURING DEVICES

Illustration

Pupil measurement

There is a mechanical device that measures changes in pupil diameter when individuals are exposed to slides showing advertisements, packages, or other stimuli by means of this specially designed equipment.

To conduct pupil dilation studies, . . . the material to be tested is prepared in 35 mm. slide form and each stimulus slide is matched for reflected illumination with a neutral control slide containing nothing but the numbers one through five. Each study usually accommodates ten stimuli, or a total of ten pairs of stimulus and control slides. . . .

The subject (individual) looks at each slide for ten seconds while his left eye is photographed at

2. M. Venkatesan, "Experimental Study of Consumer Behavior: Conformity and Independence." Reprinted from *Journal of Marketing Research*, Vol. III (November, 1966), pp. 385–386; published by the American Marketing Association.

Age .... Sex .... Sample ....

1. Was this the first time you have purchased this brand?   Yes ....   No ....

2. Do you usually purchase this brand?   Yes ....   No ....

3. Do you expect to purchase this brand again?   Yes ....   No ....

4. What did you like most about this brand? ....

5. What (if anything) did you like least about this brand? ....

....

6. Please circle the point on the scale that expresses your reaction to each pack.

   a. How well did you like the contents of the regular pack?

          terrible   poor   average   good   excellent

   b. How well did you like the contents of the sample pack?

          terrible   poor   average   good   excellent

7. If both were available for purchase the next time you went to the store, which would you buy?

   .... sample pack ....regular pack .... either .... neither

8. List three words that describe the two packs.

   a. Sample pack: ....

   b. Regular pack: ....

9. Which pack had the most in it?

   ....regular pack ....sample pack ....same

Figure 3–1. *Sample questionnaire used in the interview.* (James C. Naylor, "Deceptive Packaging: Are the Deceivers Being Deceived?", *Journal of Applied Psychology*, Vol. 46, 1962, p. 394. Copyright 1962 by the American Psychological Association, and reproduced by permission.)

the rate of two photographs per second. While looking at each control slide, the pupil diameter is primarily a function of the light value of the slide. As the matched (for light value) stimulus slide comes on, the pupil diameter may increase (as a function of greater interest) or it may decrease (as a function of lesser interest). It is this increase or decrease which is measured for each pair of control and stimulus slides.

The films are developed and each negative is projected onto a special scoring table large enough for the pupil to be measured with a ruler.

The basic measure is the percent increase or decrease in the average pupil diameter for the twenty photographs taken while viewing a stimulus slide, in comparison with the average pupil diameter for the twenty photographs taken while viewing the control slide.[3]

3. Herbert E. Krugman, "Some Applications of Pupil Measurement." Reprinted from *Journal of Marketing Research*, Vol. I (November, 1964), pp. 15–16; published by the American Marketing Association. For pictures of mechanical measuring devices and descriptions of other mechanical measuring devices, see Appendix A.

DIRECT MEASURES

Illustration

Effects of point-of-sale promotional material on sales of cantaloupes

In one experiment, the objective was to determine the relative effects of three types of point-of-sale promotional material on retail store sales of California cantaloupes. The effects of the three types of displays were observed in 12 locations of Super-Value Stores in Minneapolis.

To estimate the effects of the promotional material on the sales of cantaloupes, weekly store sales volume of cantaloupes by size was obtained for the ten-week period during which the experiment was conducted. Also weekly store traffic count was obtained from cash register sales data. In addition, weekly sales volume for substitutable fruits, such as bananas, fresh peaches, fresh grapes and water-melons, was examined.[4]

See Problems 3–1 to 3–4 at the end of this chapter, pages 39–42.

Subjects[5]

As mentioned earlier, the objective of an experiment is similar to that of any other methodology—measuring the responses of the *effects* (dependent variables) to the *causes* (independent variables). In marketing experiments, we are interested in the responses or effects of the consumers, stores, market areas, and the like. In most of our experiments, we are interested in the reaction of a sample of people or families to independent variables such as taste, product usage, advertising appeals, price changes, displays, and simulated shopping games. In many of the experiments in the literature, the samples are from college student populations. Apart from the ease of availability, college students are also buyers and consumers of many products and thus they can legitimately be the population

of interest in some studies. Generalizing from this sample, however, poses real problems.

Obviously, marketing experiments involve actions and reactions of people, but other units such as stores and market areas are involved in experimentation. Samples of stores can be used to test such variables as price, packaging, display, and promotional offers. For other problems, appropriate market areas can be selected. For example, "newspaper circulation is often much more tightly focused geographically than are the broadcast media; coupon mailings or sales-clerk training can be confined to city lines, if desired."[6]

Whether it is a sample of human population or a sample of supermarkets, the units whose actions or reactions are objects of an experiment are commonly called the "subjects" or "test units." They are formally defined as the "individuals or organizations whose responses to the experimental treatments (independent variable) are being studied."[7] Subjects are not restricted to only these as pointed out by Applebaum: "Products, materials, devices, media and methods are the test subjects in marketing experimentation."[8] The following illustrations demonstrate the type of subjects ordinarily used in marketing experiments.

Illustrations

An experimental study of the effects of information on consumer product evaluations

This study tested its hypotheses in an experimental situation involving the evaluation of two brands of men's white dress

4. Kenneth R. Farrell, "Effects of Point-of-Sale Promotional Material on Sales of Cantaloupes," *Journal of Advertising Research*, Vol. 5 (1965), pp. 8–9.

5. Size of sample and allocation of subjects are not discussed here as they depend on the sampling techniques and other criteria.

6. Seymour Banks, *Experimentation in Marketing* (New York: McGraw-Hill Book Company), copyright 1965, p. 15. Used with permission of McGraw-Hill Book Company. *Experimental treatments:* the alternatives whose effects are to be measured and compared, e.g., different package designs, self-service versus clerk service, different advertising themes.

7. *Ibid.*, p. 6.

8. William Applebaum and Richard F. Spears, "Controlled Experimentation in Marketing Research." Reprinted from *Journal of Marketing Research*, Vol. XIV (January, 1950), p. 507; published by the American Marketing Association.

shirts. Subjects for this study were: "one hundred and thirty-five *male college students* from a marketing course at the University of Minnesota *were* employed as *subjects*. Most of the subjects were experienced *buyers* and *consumers of the experimental product*."[9]

Influence of beer brand identification on taste perception

In this experiment dealing with taste perception, beer drinkers tasted beer from labeled and unlabeled bottles. Only male beer drinkers who drank beer at least three times a week were recruited as subjects. This group was composed of 326 adult drinkers who were randomly selected and who agreed to participate in the study.[10]

The consumer and his alternatives: an experimental approach

This experiment tried to investigate the relationship between the number of alternatives and decision making by consumers. The subjects were involved in choosing from alternative brands of cake mixes. Appropriately enough, the subjects for this experiment were homemakers who were members of six church groups in the twin-city area of Minneapolis–St. Paul. Twenty-four homemakers were included from each church to complete the sample requirement of 144 homemakers.[11]

Test marketing cookware coated with teflon

An experiment was designed to discover whether or not the market for non-stick cookware could be resurrected with the improved product and a

9. Donald J. Hempel, "An Experimental Study of the Effects of Information on Consumer Product Evaluations," in Raymond M. Haas (editor), *Science, Technology and Marketing*. Proceedings of the 1966 Fall Conference. (Chicago, Ill.: American Marketing Association), 1966, pp. 590–591.

10. Ralph I. Allison and Kenneth P. Uhl, "Influence of Beer Brand Identification on Taste Perception." Reprinted from *Journal of Marketing Research*, Vol. I (August, 1964), p. 36; published by the American Marketing Association.

11. Lee K. Anderson, James R. Taylor, and Robert J. Holloway, "The Consumer and His Alternatives: An Experimental Approach." Reprinted from *Journal of Marketing Research*, Vol. III (February, 1966), pp. 62–63; published by the American Marketing Association.

television consumer advertising program. If so, what level of advertising would be necessary to move the product in significant quantities? The basic design called for 13 cities to receive three levels of television advertising during the Fall of 1962 product introduction (as shown in Table 3-1).

Table 3–1. Fall 1962 product advertising*

10 daytime commercial minutes per week	5 daytime commercial minutes per week	No ads
Detroit	Dayton	Wichita
Springfield	St. Louis	Philadelphia
Columbus	Bangor	Grand Rapids
Omaha	Youngstown	Rochester
	Pittsburgh	

*James C. Becknell, Jr., and Robert W. McIsaac, "Test Marketing Cookware Coated with 'Teflon,'" *Journal of Advertising Research*, Vol. 3 (September, 1963), p. 3.

The responsiveness of food sales to supermarket shelf space changes

This experiment was to determine the relationship between shelf space and product sales—the *test units* were the *supermarkets*.

The desirability of selecting the six supermarkets randomly from all supermarkets in the area was considered. . . .

The district manager of the largest supermarket chain in Austin, Texas, was approached about using six supermarkets. Since two of the stores had crowded shelf conditions which could make testing of shelf treatments difficult, he suggested that these two stores be dropped from the experiment. Accordingly, two additional supermarkets from a local chain were added. The study was then conducted with four supermarkets from the regional chain, and two supermarkets from the local chain.[12]

See Problems 3–5 and 3–6 at the end of this chapter, pages 43 and 44.

Control of variables

In explaining the experimental method, it was noted earlier that the experiment differed from other research methods in that the experimenter has some degree of

12. Keith K. Cox, "The Responsiveness of Food Sales to Supermarket Shelf Space Changes." Reprinted from *Journal of Marketing Research*, Vol. I (May, 1964), p. 64; published by the American Marketing Association.

control over the variables. Compared to non-experimental inquiry, an experiment provides control over independent and extraneous variables and even some control over the dependent variables. The control over independent variables facilitates their variation (called manipulation) by the experimenter. This aspect of control is discussed on the following pages.

WHAT IS CONTROL?

The word *control* has three meanings: (1) a *check*, in the sense of a verification but thus also in the sense of a restraint, since verification restrains; (2) a *restraint*, in the sense of a checking and thus also in the sense of maintaining constancy; and (3) a *guide* or *directing*, in the sense of producing a precisely predetermined change, a constant and thus a restrained change. . . .

Control in the sense of restraint has always been used in experimentation to keep conditions constant and is thus an essential part of the experimental method.

Control in the sense of guidance is involved in causing an independent variable to vary in a specified and known manner and is thus also essential in experimentation.

Control in the sense of a check or comparison, the original meaning of the word, appears in all experimentation because a discoverable fact is a difference or a relation, and a discovered datum has significance only as it is related to a frame of reference, to a relatum.[13]

The importance of control over the extraneous variables can hardly be overemphasized when one considers the illustration of the brand Z gasoline presented earlier (see page 14). A simple method of control in experimentation is to create two groups—one exposed to the independent variable (called the experimental treatment) and the other group not exposed to the independent variable. The former group is called the "experimental" group and the latter is called the "control" group. The following example illustrates this point:

. . . we will consider the example of the business researcher interested in measuring the effective-

ness of an advertisement. The effectiveness will be measured as the difference in the rate of sale of the advertised product between the group exposed to the advertisement and the group not exposed. We will assume that the group exposed to the advertisement is distinguishable from the group not exposed and that actual sales to each group can be measured. These assumptions might be approximated in circumstances in which local newspaper, outdoor, or local radio advertising could be used. Under these circumstances it would be possible to advertise in some local markets while refraining from advertising in others. We will number each of the local markets and select some of them—say, twenty—by a random process such as reference to a table of random numbers. These twenty markets will then be divided into two equal groups by a random process, and one group (the experimental group) will be exposed to the advertisement for some specified length of time. The rates of sale for the two groups—"experimental" and "control" groups—will be measured for some specified length of time prior to, during, and after the exposure to advertising. Some conclusion will then be reached regarding the significance of the difference in the changes in the rates of sale to the two groups. . . .

The stimulus which was controllable and whose effect was being investigated is the advertisement. The group to be subjected to the stimulus was selected by a random process, the use of a table of random numbers. The measurements of the rates of sale were made and some conclusion was reached regarding the effect of the advertising, in spite of the fact that nothing had been done to control or measure the other factors that might have affected the rates of sale to the exposed and unexposed groups. The conclusion could be either that there was a significantly greater increase in the rate of sales in the exposed group or that there was not.[14]

Techniques of control[15]

The need for control of the extraneous variables is so paramount in an experiment that this phase of experimental planning is crucial. First the possible extraneous variables that might affect the results are

13. Edwin G. Boring, "The Nature and History of Experimental Control," *American Journal of Psychology*, Vol. 67 (December, 1954), pp. 573 and 589. Copyright 1954 by the American Psychological Association, and reproduced by permission.

14. James H. Lorie and Harry V. Roberts, "Some Comments on Experimentation in Business Research," *Journal of Business*, Vol. XXIII (April 1950), p. 97.

15 Based on F. J. McGuigan, *Experimental Psychology: A Methodological Approach*, 2nd ed. (Englewood Cliffs, N.J.: Prentice-Hall, Inc.), 1968, pp. 106-116.

determined. Then the experimenter must ascertain what control techniques are available to regulate the extraneous variables so that the effects of the independent variables can be clearly isolated. Several techniques of control are available to an experimenter; the steps are illustrated in Figure 3–2.

ELIMINATION

This is a desired control technique of extraneous variables. It eliminates the extraneous variable from the experimental situation.

Illustration

Experimental study of consumer behavior: conformity and independence

Refer to the experiment by Venkatesan in the illustration on page 30. It will be recalled that in the experimental conditions the naive subject faced three confederates of the experimenter. Thus one of the extraneous variables that might affect the response of the naive subject is his perception of competence of other subjects (confederates) in judging the suits. In order to eliminate this extraneous variable, the experimenter casually asked each of the four subjects, before the start of the task, whether any one of them has any special experience in judging men's suits or whether any one was engaged in selling men's clothing. The confederates had been instructed to answer in the negative. Thus, any "perception of experience on the part of

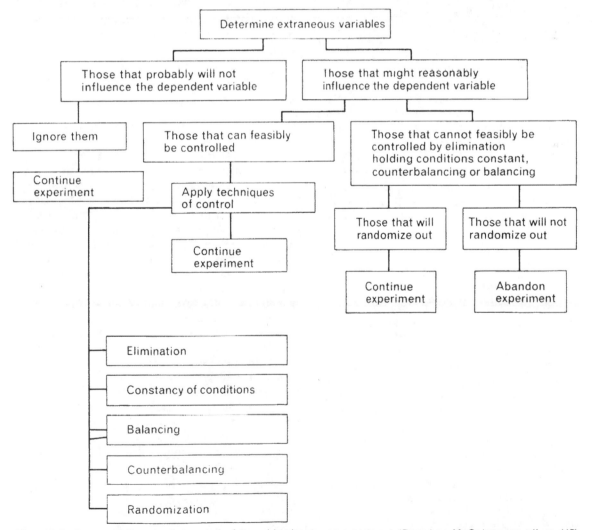

Figure 3–2. *An overall diagram of steps to be followed in planning an experiment.* (Based on McGuigan, *op. cit.,* p. 117)

other individuals" as an extraneous variable was *eliminated* from the experiment.[16]

CONSTANCY OF CONDITIONS

This technique attempts to hold the extraneous variables constant throughout the experiment. For example, if the time of day is an important extraneous variable, this control technique would require that all subjects be introduced into the experiment at approximately the same hour on successive days.

One of the standard applications of the technique of holding conditions constant is to conduct experimental sessions in the same room. Thus whatever might be the influence of the particular characteristics of the room (gayness, odors, color of the walls and furniture, location), that influence would be the same for all subjects. In like manner to hold various subject variables constant (educational level, sex, age), we need merely subjects with the characteristics that we want. . . .

Numerous characteristics of our experimental procedure must be subjected to this technique of control. Instructions to subjects, for instance, are extremely important. For this reason experimenters read precisely the same written set of instructions to all subjects (except where they must be modified for different experimental conditions) ... To exercise more precise control, then, many experimenters have all subjects listen to the same standardized instructions from a tape recorder. . . .[17]

Illustration
The relationship between shelf space and product sales in supermarkets

A problem that affected the four test products was to keep constant all factors other than shelf space throughout the testing period. In all stores, the same shelf level that existed before the tests began was maintained throughout the test period. Only the amount of shelf space (shelf treatments) was changed. Another problem involved store personnel accidentally changing shelf spaces when they restocked the test products. This distortion was minimized by auditing each store four times a week. In this way, any change could be detected in a minimum amount of time. The writer personally stocked as many of the products as possible, and

cooperation of stock clerks also helped lessen treatment deviations.[18]

BALANCING

This technique attempts to balance out the effects of extraneous variables.

If the experimental and control groups are treated in the same way except with regard to the independent variable, then any difference between the two groups on the dependent variable is ascribable to the independent variable. . . .[19]

Now you can see the implication of the illustration presented earlier of an experimental group and a control group as a simple way of controlling extraneous variables. One specific way of balancing the subjects (to control subject variables) is to match the subjects in the experimental and control conditions of the known extraneous variable to be controlled.

Illustration
And now a word from our sponsor

Some thirty-six hundred Bloomington children and Indiana University students had been involved in the clinical testing. Roughly half of them had used the new toothpaste, still unnamed, which contained stannous, or tin, fluoride. The other half had used a control toothpaste—exactly the same formula except that the fluoride was omitted. . . .

The Bloomington studies started in 1952, and Muhler described how they had been managed. After enrolling, the subjects were handed plain white tubes of toothpaste, each marked only with a small symbol—a cross, a square, a triangle, or something of the sort. Neither Muhler nor any of his associates in Bloomington knew the key to these markings. That information was restricted to an independent statistician, who worked out the results from coded report cards. . . .

Would the stannous-fluoride toothpaste do any good in ordinary homes under ordinary conditions? For that reason, the subjects were not given any instructions about how to brush their teeth, or when, or how often. They didn't even know, except in the vaguest terms, what was being investigated; a mimeographed letter explained

16. M. Venkatesan, *op. cit.*, pp. 384–387.
17. McGuigan, *op. cit.*, pp. 107–108.

18. Keith K. Cox, *The Relationship Between Shelf Space and Product Sales in Supermarkets* (Austin: Bureau of Business Research, The University of Texas), 1964, p. 20.
19. McGuigan, *op. cit.*, p. 110.

that the university was engaged in "dental research" and let it go at that.[20]

COUNTERBALANCING

This control technique is utilized when a subject is to be exposed to more than one experimental treatment. For example, if a subject is to be shown two television commercials (A and B) being tested, the technique of counterbalancing would require that half the subjects be shown commercial A first and then commercial B, whereas for the other half of the subjects, the showing order would be reversed.

Illustration

The perceived effects of piggyback television commercials

The purpose of the study was to determine the effects of "piggybacking" of television commercials. The subjects each were shown 30-second versions of two commercials.

Group AB: 30-second version of the Mustang commercial A followed by piggyback 30-second version of a food commercial (B).

Group BA: The two 30-second commercials shown to Group AB but reversed. (That is, food commercial is shown first, followed by Mustang commercial.)[21]

RANDOMIZATION

In some cases, none of the control techniques mentioned above may be utilized; if we assume that certain extraneous variables might operate in the situation but we cannot specify them, then we may assume that the extraneous variables will "randomize out." That is, it is conceivable that the effects of the extraneous variables will affect both the experimental and control groups approximately to the same extent.

20. Bruce Bliven, Jr., "And Now a Word From Our Sponsor," *The New Yorker* (March 23, 1963), pp. 86, 89–90.

21. John A. Martilla and Donald L. Thompson, "The Perceived Effects of 'Piggback' Television Commercials." Reprinted from *Journal of Marketing Research*, Vol. III (November, 1966), p. 367; published by the American Marketing Association.

Randomization techniques (such as random assignment of subjects to experimental conditions) are used not only to control extraneous variables, but also to insure the validity of statistical tests to be used in the analysis.

The potential extraneous variables that might appear in the experimental situation are considerable. Various events might occur in an unsystematic way, such as the ringing of campus bells, the clanging of radiator pipes, peculiar momentary behavior of the experimentor such as a tic, sneezing, or scratching, an outsider intruding, odors from the chemistry laboratory, and the dripping of water from an overhead pipe. Now it might be possible to anticipate many of these variables and control them with one of our techniques, but even if it is possible, it might not be feasible. Signs may be placed to head off instrusions, but signs are not always read. . . .

It really must be assumed that all such variables will not be controlled by means of the previous techniques.[22]

Illustration

Refer to the illustration by Lorie and Roberts on page 34. In this illustration the researchers were interested in the selection of 20 local markets.

We will number each of the local markets and select some of them—say, 20—by a random process such as reference to a table of random numbers. These 20 markets will then be divided into two equal groups by a random process, and one group (the experimental group) will be exposed to the advertisement for some specified length of time.[23]

See Problems 3–7 and 3–8 at the end of this chapter, pages 45 and 46.

Manipulation

Since the experimenter has some degree of of control over the independent variables, he may vary the independent variable (experimental variable) in several ways as desired. Such variation in the independent variable by the experimenter is called an "experimental treatment." This results from manipulation of the independent

22. McGuigan, *op. cit.*, pp. 115–116.
23. Lorie and Roberts, *op. cit.*, p. 97.

variables. Manipulation in an experiment is always purposive and intentional. The experimenter deliberately intervenes to influence the experimental situation.

In many experimental situations we are not interested in one independent variable, but rather in ascertaining what variations of the independent variables will produce, in terms of effects (results). In other words, the intensity and value of the independent variable are deliberately manipulated to observe the range of effects resulting from such variations. Manipulations are accomplished by physical changes such as changes in displays, variations in the shelf-space, or by changes in the instructions to the subjects. The two examples provided in the following illustrations show different manipulations.

Illustrations

Use of experimental design in the study of media effectiveness

In one experiment, it was decided to manipulate billboard advertising—the independent variable— in three ways (three treatments). Accordingly, three different sets of markets were used, (1) one receiving no advertising, (2) another receiving a $200,000 advertising campaign, and (3) another receiving a $400,000 advertising campaign. In other words, there is a $200,000 campaign of bill-boards put into cities in experimental situation 2, a $400,000 campaign of billboards put into cities in experimental situation 3, and no advertising in one group of cities (Control Situation).

Control situation 1	*Experimental situation 2*	*Experimental situation 3*
No advertising	Some advertising	Much advertising[24]

24. James C. Becknell, Jr., "Use of Experimental Design in the Study of Media Effectiveness," *Media/ Scope* (August, 1962), pp. 46–49.

An experimental study of customer effort, expectation and statisfaction

Refer to this illustration on page 13. The two independent variables, effort and expectation, were manipulated as follows:

Expectation was manipulated by the use of two 31-item catalogs in the study. Both contained descriptions and prices of ball-point pens of the type usually purchased by the subjects. The high expectation catalog contained products whose median price was about $1.95. The products shown in the low expectation catalog were priced between 29¢ and 59¢; the average price was about 39¢. All subjects received the same 39¢ pen, ostensibly chosen by lot from the samples provided by the manufacturers whose products were shown in the catalog. Thus, the rational expectation of a student who saw the high expectation catalog was a $1.95 writing instrument; of a student who used the low expectation catalog, a 39¢ pen.

Effort was manipulated by a simulated shopping task. The task required low effort subjects to look through one of the catalogs as if shopping, and to write down one feature which impressed them for half of the items shown. This minimum effort procedure took about 15 minutes. High effort subjects worked about an hour in uncomfortable surroundings. They were asked to comb one catalog carefully, and to record five different features about each of the 31 items. The purpose of their task was to force them to invest considerable shopping effort.[25]

See Problems 3–9 and 3–10 at the end of this chapter, pages 47 and 48.

25. Richard N. Cardozo, "An Experimental Study of Customer Effort, Expectation and Satisfaction," *Journal of Marketing Research*, Vol. II (August, 1965), pp. 245–246.

Name	Instructor
Date	Section

Problem 3–1

In one experiment, the experimenter called at the homes of the 42 participants twice a week for eight weeks. Each of the 42 women in the study was shown four brands of bread which were placed on a tray so that the participant could easily see and choose the one she wanted. Each was given her choice of the four brands of bread.

Identify the measure used in this study: _____

_____

_____

_____

_____

Problem 3–2

Refer to the experiment on "Customary prices" (see page 2). What was the measure used to determine the effects of customary prices? _____

_____

_____

_____

_____

_____

Problem 3–3

In a study investigating the flavor preference for a brand of coffee, the following method of measurement was employed.*

	1	2	3	4	THE BRAND OF COFFEE I PREFER TO USE	5	THE BRAND OF COFFEE I PREFER TO USE	6	7	8	9	
Lighter appearance in the cup	☐	☐	☐	☐		☐		☐	☐	☐	☐	Darker appearance in the cup
Flavor of a weaker blend	☐	☐	☐	☐		☐		☐	☐	☐	☐	Flavor of a stronger blend
Less bitterness	☐	☐	☐	☐		☐		☐	☐	☐	☐	More bitterness
Less aroma in the cup	☐	☐	☐	☐		☐		☐	☐	☐	☐	More aroma in the cup
A less roasted flavor in the cup	☐	☐	☐	☐		☐		☐	☐	☐	☐	A more roasted flavor in the cup
Lighter body	☐	☐	☐	☐		☐		☐	☐	☐	☐	Heavier body
Poorer flavor in the cup	☐	☐	☐	☐		☐		☐	☐	☐	☐	Better flavor in the cup
Lighter color of grounds in the can	☐	☐	☐	☐		☐		☐	☐	☐	☐	Darker color of grounds in the can

What is the measure? _____

_____

_____

_____

_____

*J. O. Eastlack, Jr., "Consumer Flavor Preference Factors in Food Product Design." Reprinted from *Journal of Marketing Research*, Vol. I (February, 1964), p. 40; published by the American Marketing Association.

Name _____   Instructor _____

Date _____   Section _____

Problem 3-4

What type of measures would you use in the following situations?

1. Effectiveness of displays in a supermarket

_____

_____

_____

2. Changes in price for a brand of cake mix

_____

_____

_____

3. Preference for a flavor of ice cream

_____

_____

_____

4. Attitude toward beer-drinking

_____

_____

_____

5. Satisfaction with a purchase

_____

_____

_____

6. Certainty for a choice of hair spray

_____

_____

_____

Name   Instructor

Date   Section

Problem 3-5

The Gem Company has been directing some of its advertising research along the lines outlined in the chart below. The experiment was designed to determine the sales and profit
response to advertising.

Multi-media experimental design (numbers are area designations)

	NO NEWSPAPERS				NEWSPAPERS			
	No radio		Radio		No radio		Radio	
	No TV	TV	No TV	TV	No TV	TV	No TV	TV
No outdoor advertising	1	2	3	4	5	6	7	8
Outdoor advertising	9	10	11	12	13	14	15	16

1. Identify the subjects of this experiment:

2. What are the independent variables?

3. How was the response (dependent variable) measured?

Problem 3-6

An experiment is designed to test the responses to price changes for a brand of cake mix. The schedules of prices to be tested are determined in advance, and they are assigned to the test periods on a random basis. Results of this experiment will be measured in terms of actual sales of the test brand of caked mix during the test periods.

Identify the test units involved in this experiment and explain the reasons for your answer.

_____

_____

_____

_____

_____

_____

Name   Instructor

Date   Section

Problem 3-7

An experimenter wanted to determine the effect that special mail promotional material pertaining to eggs had on egg purchases of selected families. The procedure was to analyze changes in egg purchases for groups of families. Each group received a different number and kind of promotional material. What control problems do you see in such an experiment and how would you handle them?

Problem 3–8

Refer to Problem 1–6 on page 10. This problem gave you the details of a study on shopping cart displays. How would you improve the controls involved in this study?

_____

_____

_____

_____

_____

_____

_____

_____

Name	Instructor
Date	Section

Problem 3–9

An experiment was set up to determine the effects of changes in the relationship between the prices of skim milk and whole milk on skim milk sales. The experiment consisted of a random assignment of skim milk price differentials over a four-year period with each yearly period divided into four bimonthly subperiods. (The experiment ran from October through May of each year with a price preperiod in September.) The exact price pattern is given by the complete experimental design which follows:*

	Year I	Year II	Year III	Year IV
Preperiod	*(A)*	*(B)*	*(D)*	*(C)*
Subperiod				
1	A	B	D	C
2	B	D	C	A
3	C	A	B	D
4	D	C	A	B

The capital letters having the following significance:

A = 6¢ differential
B = 2¢ differential
C = 4¢ differential
D = 8¢ differential

What is the experimental variable? _____

How is it manipulated? _____

*Donald J. Baker and Charles H. Berry, "The Price Elasticity of Demand for Fluid Skim Milk," *Journal of Farm Economics*, Vol. XXXV (February, 1953), pp. 124–129.

Problem 3–10

In one experiment, dealing with buying situations, the experimenter gave two sets of instructions. Instructions No. 1 to group A and Instructions No. 2 to group B, as indicated below:

Instructions No. 1 (To Group A)

You have been in northern Minnesota for the weekend and are driving back to the Twin Cities. After a stop for coffee, you find that you cannot start the engine of your car. You return to the restaurant and locate the phone number of a nearby garage. The attendant arrives in a few minutes, checks your car, and reports that your battery probably has a leaky cell which is shorting out. The attendant tows your car into his garage and determines that your battery is dead and cannot be recharged. The long winter has apparently taken its toll.

Instructions No. 2 (To Group B)

You were planning on running several errands today. After the first stop, however, your car will not start. After several attempts to start it, you give up and call the nearest garage. The attendant arrives in a few minutes and starts your car with the aid of his booster battery.

You follow him to his garage where he checks over your engine and battery. He believes that you may have a leaky cell in the battery and that, with a little luck, it may be possible for you to get along for a few weeks.

1. What is the variable the experimenter is trying to manipulate? _____

2. In how many ways is it manipulated? _____

3. Label the manipulations: _____

4

Ingredients—design aspects

Design aspects

Having considered the problems of measurement, subjects, control, and manipulation of variables, we are now ready to consider (1) design aspects, including experimental design, and (2) experimental techniques and procedures. At the end of this chapter, an example is provided to illustrate the series of steps involved in conducting an experiment.

... In any experiment, control over all possible variables affecting the response is rarely, if ever, possible. Even in the laboratory it is not possible to control *all* variables which could conceivably affect the outcome. But compared to the laboratory situation, the researcher who is working in the market place has a really difficult control job on his hands. In real-world market experimentation, it is not possible to come even close to holding other factors constant. Rather, the market researcher must try to design his experiment so that the effects of uncontrolled variables do not obscure and bias the nature of the response which he is attempting to ascertain in the variables which *are* being controlled.

An illustration should make this point clear. Suppose a marketing researcher is interested in conducting a series of taste-testing experiments for a new soft drink. Subjective interpretations of, say, "sweetness" may well vary from subject to subject. If half the subjects were asked to taste only an established soft drink brand and the other half were asked to taste only the new brand, the average "sweetness" rating could reflect mainly the inherent subjective differences between each group of subjects. A preferable procedure might be to have each subject taste each of the two drinks on the assumption that intrasubject expressions of "sweetness" will affect each response approximately equally; that is, ratings will be expressed in terms of *differences* in "sweetness" over each subject. To avoid "ordering" effects on responses, the new and the control drink would be presented in randomized order. To reduce "carry-over" tendencies, the subject would be asked, say, to take a sip of water between tasting trials.'

In the preceding illustration, it is clear that statistical techniques are needed to avoid ordering effects and to reduce carry-over effects. These and similar problems arising in experimentation are handled by statistical techniques known as experimental design; its objective is to achieve optimum statistical efficiency in the design of experiments. A discussion of the technical aspects of the statistical control of experiments is beyond the scope of this book. However, the illustrations provided in this section offer a clear view of some of the designs which are frequently used in marketing experimentation and the reasons for such designs. For example, in the taste-testing illustration above, the use of randomization will decidedly affect the "ordering" effects on responses. Other techniques, such as "matching" the subjects in the experimental and control groups in their characteristics and obtaining before-and-after measurements, may be used to reduce the variation resulting from extraneous and other controlled factors.

Experimental designs

An experimental design is a specific plan for research having certain statistical and logical qualities. There are various types of designs, each having certain attributes, levels of efficiency, and developed for specific purposes. In most problems where the experimental design is considered as a measurement tool, the research is basically interested in a comparison of the relative efficiency of alternatives. For example, how well does one promotional appeal, say health, sell milk as compared with other appeals, such as refreshment, etc.? Through the chosen design, a measurement is taken of the sales efficiency of the alternatives

1. Paul E. Green and Donald S. Tull, *Research for Marketing Decisions*, © 1966, p. 373. Reprinted by permission of Prentice-Hall, Inc., Englewood Cliffs, New Jersey.

tested in such a fashion that nothing in the experiment itself favors one alternative over another. There are many different types of designs some simple, others complex.[2]

The following examples illustrate the different types of designs used in marketing experimentation. These are rather simple designs, and students desiring complex designs should familiarize themselves with the area of statistically designed experiments.[3]

The following classification may help the student in understanding some of the basic differences in experimental designs.

One variable manipulated	More than one variable manipulated
Randomized designs	Factorial designs
Randomized blocks	
Latin square	
Carry-over designs	

BEFORE-AFTER DESIGNS

After-only designs

This design[4] can be illustrated as follows:

	Experimental group
1. Experimental variable introduced	Yes
2. "After" measurement	Yes (X_1)
Effect of experimental variable $= X_1$	

	After
Experimental group	X_1

As its name suggests, a "before-after" design does not require prior measurement. In this design, the subjects are exposed to the experimental variable (treatment) and then the dependent measure is taken. There is no control group.

Illustration

Roe herring is a traditional breakfast dish in Virginia, but in modern times is not widely eaten.

2. William S. Hoofnagle, "Experimental Designs in Measuring the Effectiveness of Promotion." Reprinted from *Journal of Marketing Research*, Vol. II (May, 1965), p. 154; published by the American Marketing Association.

3. Much of this section, including the designs, is taken from Harper W. Boyd and Ralph Westfall, *Marketing Research: Text and Cases*, Revised edition (Homewood, Ill.: Richard D. Irwin, Inc.), 1964, pp. 95–106. Students are referred to this excellent material.

4. Modified from *ibid.*, p. 96.

In an attempt to widen the market, the firm owning Tidewater brand ran an advertisement in the Sunday morning Richmond newspaper and in both the morning and evening newspapers during the following six days. This ad carried a coupon which could be exchanged at a grocery store for one free can of Tidewater roe herring. A total of 46,486 free cans were so claimed.[5]

After-only-with-control design

The experimental and control groups are selected in such a way as to be equivalent. No "before" measurement is made in either group. The effect of the experimental variable is determined by computing the difference between the two "after" measurements ($X_1 - Y_1$).[6]

The design can be illustrated as follows:

	Experimental group	Control group
1. Before measurement	No	No
2. Experimental variable	Yes	No
3. After measurement	Yes (X_1)	Yes (Y_1)
Effect of experimental variable $= X_1 - Y_1$		

	After
Experimental group	X_1
Control group	Y_1

Illustration

This involves doing something to one group of people or one group of markets and not doing the same thing to another.

Let us assume we plan to put a billboard advertising campaign into a marketing plan. Our management wants to know if this is going to increase sales at all, and if it does increase sales is it worth the additional cost. Ideally, to test this we will take a selection of 100 markets, totally isolated from one another, and on a random basis put billboards in 50 of the markets and no billboards in the other 50. If we want to be slightly more sophisticated about it, we will previously rank the markets from 1 to 100, and then randomly assign every other market to either the billboard situation or the no-billboard situation. By a random assignment here I mean that for every two markets we flip a coin to see which one goes where; we do not put the biggest in billboard condition; the second

5. Alan S. Donnahoe, "The Great Roe Herring Experiment" (Richmond, Virginia: *Richmond-Times Dispatch*), undated.

6. Boyd and Westfall, *op. cit.*, p. 109.

in the no-billboard; the third, billboard; fourth, no-billboard; etc.[7]

Before-After-without-control design

In this design, the experimenter measures the dependent variable before exposing the subjects to the experimental variable and after exposing the subjects to the experimental variable. The difference between the two is considered to be a measurement of the effect of the experimental variable.

This can be illustrated as follows:[8]

	Experimental group
1. Before measurement	Yes (X_1)
2. Experimental variables introduced	Yes
3. After measurement	Yes (X_2)

Effect of experimental variable $= X_2 - X_1$

	Before	After
Experimental group	X_1	X_2

Illustration

Schwerin Research Corporation used the "before-after" design in its testing of TV commercials. A group of consumers in a theater is told that a drawing is to be held; the winner will receive, for example, $10 worth of hair spray. Each consumer is to check on a card which of a list of major hair spray brands she would like if she should win. The drawing is held. Next, the consumers are shown a thirty-minute movie in which three different commercials are interspersed. One commercial is for a given brand of hair spray. After the movie, another drawing is held. Each consumer indicates the brand of hair spray she wants if she should win this second drawing. Schwerin counts the number requesting the brand promoted by the hair spray commercial. The difference between the percentage of consumers wanting the brand in the second drawing and in the first drawing is a measure of the effectiveness of the commercial.[9]

Before-After-with-control design

This is the ideal model of a controlled experiment, as the following diagram illustrates.[10]

7. James C. Becknell, Jr., "Use of Experimental Design in the Study of Media Effectiveness," *Media/Scope* (August, 1962), p. 47.

8. Boyd and Westfall, *op. cit.*, p. 98.

9. *Ibid.*

10. *Ibid.*, p. 101.

	Experimental group	Control group
1. Before measurement	Yes (X_1)	Yes (Y_1)
2. Experimental variable	Yes	No
3. After measurement	Yes (X_2)	Yes (Y_2)

Effect of experimental variable $= (X_2 - X_1) - (Y_2 - Y_1)$

	Before	After
Experimental group	X_1	X_2
Control group	Y_1	Y_2

First, comparable experimental and control groups are selected. Before measurements are obtained from both groups. The experimental variable is then introduced in only the experimental group. Subsequently, after measurements are made for both groups.

Illustration

An experiment run by the National Broadcasting Company illustrates this design. A carefully selected sample of 2,441 male and female household heads in a medium-sized midwestern market was interviewed at two different times three months apart. Purchases during the preceding four-week period of twenty-two different brands in eleven different household product categories varying from beer to toothpaste were determined in each of the two interviews. In the first interview, the percentage buying one or more of the brands was determined for the entire sample and used as the "before" measure. In the second interview, the sample was separated into two sub-samples —those exposed to TV and magazine advertising of the products and those not exposed to the advertising. The results were as follows:[11]

	Experimental group (exposed to advertising)	Control group (not exposed to advertising)
1. "Before" measurement (percentage purchasing in past 4 weeks)	19.4 (X_1)	19.4 (Y_1)
2. Experimental variable (exposed to advertising of products)	Yes	No
3. "After" measurement (percentage purchasing in past 4 weeks at time of second interview)	20.5 (X_2)	16.9 (Y_2)

Effect of experimental variable $= (20.5\% - 19.4\%) - (16.9\% - 19.4\%) = (1.1\%) - (-2.5\%) = 3.6\%$

See Problems 4–1 and 4–2 at the end of this chapter, pages 63 and 64.

11. *Ibid.*, pp. 101–102.

Time periods	STORES			
	1	2	3	4
1	Red mesh	Purple mesh	Purple mesh	Purple mesh
2	Red mesh	Polyethylene	Paper	Polyethylene
3	Red mesh	Paper	Polyethylene	Paper
4	Red mesh	Polyethylene	Purple mesh	Paper

RANDOMIZED DESIGNS

Completely randomized designs

This is a simple design in which treatments are assigned randomly to subjects or test units involved in the experiment. That is, any number of treatments can be assigned by a random process to any number of experimental units.[12]

Illustration

In an experiment to test the effects of four types of packaging material (four treatments) on apple sales, a completely randomized design was used. Test units were four stores; four time periods were used to test the four packaging materials: red mesh, purple mesh, paper, and polyethylene. Since the treatments are assigned at random, one possible arrangement of a completely randomized design may be as shown above.[13]

In the preceding illustration, four stores, four time periods, and four treatments are used. This is not a requirement of a completely randomized design; the appearance of the same number of stores, same number of time periods, and same number of treatments is a sheer coincidence.

Randomized block design

A completely randomized design, such as the preceding one, is of very limited use in marketing experimentation, as we are faced with complex situations. For example, in the illustration above, the design must assume that the test stores are of equal size; otherwise, the size of the store itself may be a significant variable affecting the results.

12. See page 32 for definition of "treatments."
13. Peter L. Henderson, *Methods of Research in Marketing: Paper No. 3. Application of the Double Change-over Design to Measure Carry-over Effects of Treatments in Controlled Experiments.* Ithaca, N.Y.: Department of Agricultural Economics, Cornell University Agricultural Experiment Station, New York State College of Agriculture, Cornell University (July, 1951), p. 4.

Likewise, the time periods used may also have unequal effects. "The possibility can readily be seen that neither stores nor time would have equal influences on all treatments in a completely randomized design using only a limited number of stores over a short period of time."[14]

In the completely randomized design shown above, both the variables (stores and time) are uncontrollable, as the only requirement for this design is that the treatments be assigned at random to test units. In such a situation, an improvement in the design is brought about by a *randomized block* design which places some restrictions on the random assignment of treatments. Suppose that an experimenter is interested in the effects of three types of display racks (treatments) on the effect of sales. Since the influence of the size of store needs to be controlled, the test units (stores) can be grouped in terms of size; then the treatments can be assigned randomly to each group. Each group now consists of homogeneous test units. Stores are now "blocks." Thus, the design would eliminate the effect of one uncontrollable variable—store size. In a randomized block design, then, subjects are exposed to the experimental variables (treatments) in a restricted fashion. The objective is to divide the subjects into a number of groups or blocks, each of which has relatively homogeneous experimental units in it. Each block or group is then considered a replication. The term *randomized block* is derived from agricultural experiments in which a unit (subject) for experimentation is a plot of land and a block consists of adjoining plots. The plots nearer to one another are homogeneous (alike) in some respects—such as condition of the soil, fertility, and the like.

14. *Ibid.*, pp. 3–4.

Similarly, for example, we may have reason to believe that in marketing experiments dealing with shelf spaces, displays, packaging material, and so on, stores of the same size can be grouped together in "blocks" in order to assess the effects of the independent variables for the "blocks."

Illustration

In an experiment, the objective was to test the effectiveness of three types of display racks: end-aisle displays, gondola displays, and check-out stand racks.

Eighteen test stores were made available: they were divided into three groups on the basis of size. Each treatment was assigned at random to two stores within each size group, and a different randomization was made for each group. These racks were used during the Friday and Saturday of a single week, and sales were measured by auditing the contents at the beginning and end of the test period.[15]

The design was as follows:

| Treatment | STORE | | |
	Large	Medium	Small
End-aisle	2 stores	2 stores	2 stores
Gondola	2 stores	2 stores	2 stores
Check-out stand	2 stores	2 stores	2 stores

See Problems 4–3 and 4–4 at the end of this chapter, pages 65 and 66.

LATIN SQUARES

Many times, we are interested in isolating the effects of various factors from each other. For example, if we are interested in the effectiveness of window displays on the sale of turkeys, it is conceivable that the results (sales) may be affected by the day of the week and by differences in the size of the stores involved. These two principal variables may represent major sources of variations; it is thus desirable to design to remove their effects when the experiment

is being planned. We saw that randomized block design may be able to eliminate one uncontrollable variable. However, simultaneous double elimination of the two sources of variation can be accomplished only by a Latin square arrangement of the design. Eliminating these two variables as sources of variation will lead to a more accurate measure of the effects (sales) resulting from window displays (experimental variables).

Conventionally, the principal variables, whose effects we are trying to eliminate, are arranged along rows and columns. In the Latin square design, the number of treatments (exposure to a different level of experimental variable) must equal the number of rows and columns. The design calls for a diagonal square.

For n treatments, this design requires n columns, n rows and n^2 test units (hence its name). Conventionally, a square is described in terms of its number of rows and columns, 3×3, 4×4, etc. An illustration of a 4×4 Latin square with the capital letters representing treatments is illustrated below. Because each row or column represents a different sequence of the treatments, the Latin square is often used in a situation where each test unit will be exposed to all treatments and where we wish to control for a possible order effect.[16]

Suppose we wish to test four displays and want to control simultaneously the effects of two principal variables: time period and store size. The Latin square design for this experiment will have four treatments (four displays, labeled A, B, and C, D); the four time periods will appear in the rows, and the stores, grouped by size, will appear as the columns. Each treatment (display) will appear only once in each row and each column, as shown in the following table:

| Period | STORE SIZE | | | |
	1	2	3	4
I	A	B	D	C
II	D	C	A	B
III	C	D	B	A
IV	B	A	C	D

15. Seymour Banks, *Experimentation in Marketing* (New York: McGraw-Hill Book Company), copyright 1965, pp. 80–81. Used with permission of McGraw-Hill Book Company. The reader should be warned that the use of the same number of groups and treatments is purely coincidental and not a requirement of the randomized block design.

16. *Ibid.*, p. 115.

Illustration: Florida orange study

The study was conducted in selected retail supermarkets in two cities. Cleveland, Ohio, was selected to represent reactions of consumers to natural-color Florida oranges in markets which sell Florida oranges predominantly with color added. Philadelphia, Pa., was chosen to reflect Eastern markets, through which most natural-color Florida oranges are distributed.

Controlled experiments were conducted under normal retail conditions using centrally managed chain outlets in each city to minimize effects of different merchandising policies on sales of the test fruit. In Cleveland, the same 15 stores were used in each experiment. During the first experiment in Philadelphia, nine supermarkets were used. Six of these nine supermarkets were used in both the second and third experiments.

The overall study consisted of three experiments, each of 3 weeks duration. Experiments I and II were conducted in November and December of 1959 and 1960 using the Hamlin variety of oranges. The third experiment was undertaken in June 1961 using Valencia oranges.

A Latin-square experimental design was used to assign treatments to stores and time periods in both cities (Table 4–1). During any given week, consumers were given a choice of one of the three purchasing alternatives in each store—natural-color Florida oranges only, color-added only, or a combination display of both types. Each method tested was in one-third of the test stores in each city during every week of each 3-week period. Use of this type of experimental design equalizes effects on sales resulting from time and store differences.[17]

See Problems 4–5 and 4–6 at the end of this chapter, pages 67 and 68.

CARRY-OVER DESIGNS

One of the important considerations in the design of marketing experiments is that the effects of the test variables, such as price, packaging, or displays, are carried over beyond the period in which the treatments are tested. In the Latin square design illustration and problems it is possible that there may be complications, namely, that the effects of a particular display will not occur

17. Nick Havas, Michael G. Van Dress, Harold R. Lindstrom, and Pauline Kartalos, *Consumer Acceptance of Florida Oranges With and Without Color Added.* Marketing Research Report No. 537. Washington, D.C.: U.S. Department of Agriculture, Economic Research Service (May, 1962), pp. 2–3.

Table 4–1. Schedule of displays of Florida oranges with and without color added, in selected stores in Philadelphia, Pa., and Cleveland, Ohio.*

City and store number	First week	Second week	Third week
Philadelphia			
1	A	C	B
2	B	A	C
3	C	B	A
4	B	A	C
5	C	B	A
6	A	C	B
7	C	B	A
8	A	C	B
9	B	A	C
Cleveland			
1	A	C	B
2	C	B	A
3	B	A	C
4	A	C	B
5	B	A	C
6	C	B	A
7	C	A	B
8	A	B	C
9	B	C	A
10	B	A	C
11	C	B	A
12	A	C	B
13	B	C	A
14	A	B	C
15	C	A	B

*A = Color added
B = Natural color
C = Combination of A and B

immediately; some consumers may buy immediately and others may buy during the next period or even after two or three time periods. Likewise, in the problem dealing with the effectiveness of sales promotion of different-sized packages to be tested, it is possible that a particular-sized package in one time period may have beneficial or detrimental effects on sales in the next time period. Similarly, a lower price treatment or a heavy promotion treatment in one time period may have beneficial effects on the treatments that follow. In other words, there may be lingering or carry-over effects.

The use of limited time periods in Latin square designs poses problems in measuring the effect of a treatment applied in one period that extends into subsequent periods. Through a Latin square design alone, it is not possible to measure the amount of carry-over effect. In order to measure the carry-over effect, several assumptions have to be made and many changes in the Latin square designs are needed. A design that takes this carry-over effect into account is called the "double change-over" design. The double change-over design consists of reversing the sequence of treatments in two orthogonal Latin squares, as illustrated below:[18]

Time period	TEST UNITS					
	I	*II*	*III*	*IV*	*V*	*VI*
1	A	B	C	A	B	C
2	B(a)	C(b)	A(c)	C(a)	A(b)	B(c)
3	C(b)	A(c)	B(a)	B(c)	C(a)	A(b)

The small letters appearing in parentheses indicate the treatment whose lingering effect may be included in the current time period and treatment. Sometimes an extra time period is added to get better measurement of the carry-over effect. The following milk promotion study provides an example of the addition of an extra time period.

Illustration: Milk promotion study

The purpose of the experiment was to obtain an indication of the effect of varying levels of promotional intensity on sales of fluid milk. Treatments being tested reflect changes in expenditures per capita for promotion within the markets. The per capita expenditure ranges from the present (or control) level of about 2 cents to 15 cents as a medium level, and a heavy promotion.

One of the important considerations in a study of effectiveness of sales promotion is the question of carry-over of effect beyond the period in which the expenditure is actually made. This characteristic of the promotional effect requires certain refinements in the measurement technique. Provisions must be made for measuring the immediate influence plus the influence which continues in subsequent periods after the expenditure has been made.

Two alterations were made in the basic Latin square design to deal with the problem of carry-over influence. First, the design was altered to a double change-over design in which the treatment sequence is reversed in the second square (see table). Second, a fourth time period was added. With this arrangement, each promotional expenditure level is preceded by itself and every other expenditure level in the study. The capital letters in the table represent the expenditure levels. The corresponding small letters in parentheses represent the sales of markets having these expenditure levels in the previous period. The analysis of sales associated with these small letters provides an indication of the carry-over influence. The carry-over influence could be estimated with only three periods but the addition of the fourth period allows every expenditure level to follow itself and adds precision to the estimate of the carry-over effects.[19]

See Problems 4–7 and 4–8 at the end of this chapter, pages 69 and 70.

FACTORIAL DESIGNS

We saw in earlier designs that more than one factor, or one independent variable, is involved in marketing experiments. It was also observed that occasionally isolation of effects of these factors from each other was our major concern. Similarly, we may be interested in determining the effects of a combination of experimental variables. An experimental design that takes into account all possible combinations of the variables or factors is called a *factorial design*. In this design, each independent variable or factor is varied in two or more ways, called *levels*.

Suppose an experiment is concerned with

Time period	SQUARE I			SQUARE II		
	Chattanooga	*Knoxville*	*Rochester*	*Clarksburg*	*Sioux Falls*	*Neosho Valley*
1	A	B	C	A	B	C
2	B(a)	C(b)	A(c)	C(a)	A(b)	B(c)
3	C(b)	A(c)	B(a)	B(c)	C(a)	A(b)
4	C(c)	A(a)	B(b)	B(b)	C(c)	A(a)

Expenditure levels (treatments):
  A = Normal promotion (approximately 2¢ per capita annually)
  B = Medium promotion (15¢ per capita annually above normal)
  C = Heavy promotion (30¢ per capita annually above normal)

18. Two Latin squares are termed orthogonal if, when one is super-imposed upon the other, every ordered pair of symbols occurs exactly once and only once in the resulting square. (Hoofnagle, *op. cit.*, p. 157.)

19. Wendell E. Clements, Peter L. Henderson, and Cleveland P. Eley, *The Effect of Different Levels of Promotional Expenditures on Sales of Fluid Milk.* Washington, D.C.: United States Department of Agriculture, Economic Research Service, ERS-259 (October, 1965), pp. 7–8.

the effects on sales of price and color of the package design. Let us designate these two variables as variable A and variable B. Let price (A) be varied in two ways (e.g., 29¢ and 31¢) which will be indicated as A_1 and A_2. The package design (B) variable is also varied in two levels (ways): red color design (B_1) and green color design (B_2). For this example, we have four combinations, as indicated in the following factorial design:

Price	Package design	
	Red	*Green*
29¢	combination A_1 B_1	combination A_1 B_2
31¢	combination A_2 B_1	combination A_2 B_2

In factorial designs, it is conventional (as in Latin square designs) to indicate the number of factors and the number of levels of variations for each factor. For example, a $3 \times 2 \times 2$ factorial design means there are three factors; the first factor is varied in three ways, the second factor is varied in two ways, and the third factor is varied in two levels. The illustration above is a 2×2 factorial design.

A factorial design permits combination of treatments. This means we can test several factors simultaneously and also study the interrelations of several factors. Through the use of factorial designs, we can determine the main effects—in the price-package design example, the effects of and differences between the two factors. In addition, it would permit evaluations of *interactions* between the two factors. In general, the use of a factorial design facilitates the analysis of the effects in terms of *main effects* and *interactions*. The following instructions clearly demonstrate the use of factorial designs in marketing experimentation.

Illustration: an experiment in dissonance
Leon Festinger's book on cognitive dissonance touched off research in social psychology which soon spread to consumer behavior.

The consumer is constantly receiving various kinds of information from many sources such as friends, advertisements, and salesmen. These pieces of information are cognitions which, according to the theory, the consumer likes to have consistent with one another. If cognitions are inconsistent there is pressure on the consumer to reduce this inconsistency; that is to reduce dissonance. Dissonance is a post decision force, so the consumer reduces dissonance *after* he has made a buying decision. Thus a consumer who selects Brand A over all other brands may experience dissonance because there are cognitions which cause him to recognize attractive features of the rejected brands. One way for the consumer to reduce dissonance is to read advertisements of Brand A which would reinforce his buying decision. There is clearly a number of ways in which dissonance might be caused in buying situations. In actual practice, the consumer may be affected by several different factors which interact with one another, or factor "a" may dominate in one situation and factor "b" in another case. The ultimate effect depends upon the relevance of the factors in the actual buying environment. The consumer may reduce his dissonance in a number of ways. He may, for example, change his evaluations, beliefs, and opinions in order to realign his dissonant cognitions. Thus, his preference for the chosen product may increase and his opinion of the rejected may be lowered. A second way is to select information which supports his decision. The reading of automobile advertisements of the chosen auto is such an example. Ignoring cancer information is a way to reduce or avoid dissonance on the part of the cigarette smoker. A person might distort his perceptions in some way in order to reduce the feeling of dissonance. He may engage in a behavioral change of some kind. In short, the theory states that dissonance will occur under certain conditions and that there will be pressure to reduce it.

Since there was a desire to make the experience as realistic as possible, a design was chosen which embodied four factors expected to produce dissonance. Automobile batteries were chosen as the product to be involved in the buying decision because they seemed to fit into a variety of purchase situations as required.

The four factors chosen for the experiment were as follows:

A. Inducement to buy
   (1) high condition
   (2) low condition
B. Anticipated dissonance
   (1) high condition
   (2) low condition
C. Information
   (1) additional information given
   (2) no information given

Table 4–2. Example of one condition: High inducement, low anticipated dissonance, additional information, low cognitive overlap.

HIGH INDUCEMENT				LOW INDUCEMENT			
HIGH ANTICIPATED DISSONANCE		LOW ANTICIPATED DISSONANCE		HIGH ANTICIPATED DISSONANCE		LOW ANTICIPATED DISSONANCE	
No additional information	Additional information	No additional information	Additional information	No additional information	Additional information	No additional information	Additional information
Cognitive overlap	Cognitive overlap	Cognitive overlap	Cognitive overlap	Cognitive overlap	Cognitive overlap	Cognitive overlap	Cognitive overlap
High | Low	High | Low	High | Low	High | Low	High | Low	High | Low	High | Low	High | Low

D. Cognitive overlap
   (1) high condition
   (2) low condition

An experiment with four factors and two conditions in each factor meant that there would be 16 different cells in the study. The design is shown in Table 4–2. By using 80 subjects it was possible to have five subjects in each of the 16 cells. Using a factorial design, it was possible to have a sample size of 40 for each of the four main conditions.[20]

See Problems 4-9 and 4-10 at the end of this chapter, pages 71 and 72.

Experimental procedure

It was stated at the beginning of this chapter that all phases of an experiment should be carefully planned in advance. How the subjects will be exposed to treatments, how the variables will be measured, how the control techniques will be employed, and myriad other details must be planned before an experiment is conducted. In fact, the experimenter must make an outline of each point involved in the data collection process. This, of course, is like any well-conducted research, be it survey or other method. In this outline, he might start from the arrangements of the "props" before the subjects arrive at the experimental scene and follow through all the steps to the end of the experiment. This includes the setting of the experiment, physical arrangements, apparatus and their operation, data collection forms, instructions, recording of the dependent variable, greetings of subjects, dress of the experimenter, and so on.

CONDUCTING AN EXPERIMENT— AN ILLUSTRATION

Planning all phases of the experimental procedure involves planning all the components of an experiment. It would be easier to illustrate experimental procedures by showing an example of how to conduct an experiment. Consider the following example, which explains how Taylor conducted his experiment.[21]

Number of alternatives and decision making

Consumer buying process involves choice among different products or brands, or simply it is a choice among alternatives.

A number of psychological experiments investigated the relationship between the number of stimulus objects a subject has to choose from and the nature of his selection. These experiments demonstrated that when subjects are repeatedly required to predict the occurrence of two stimulus objects, they predict the occurrence of the objects in the same proportions as they were presented to the subjects.

Based on the findings by psychologists, Taylor raised the following question: If consumer goods were used as the stimulus objects and homemakers were used as subjects would the same results be observed?

To answer this question, he formulated the following hypotheses:

20. Based on the unpublished report of this experiment and the following: Robert J. Holloway, "An Experiment on Consumer Dissonance." Reprinted from *Journal of Marketing*, Vol. XXXI (January, 1967), pp. 39, 41; published by the American Marketing Association.

21. This illustration is based on Taylor's unpublished report of the experiment and on the following: Lee K. Anderson, James R. Taylor, and Robert J. Holloway, "The Consumer and His Alternatives: An Experimental Approach," *Journal of Marketing Research*, Vol. III (February, 1966), pp. 63–64.

Hypothesis 1

In a multiple alternative situation where one alternative is presented as correct more frequently than the others, predicting the occurrence of the more frequently occurring alternative is independent of the number of alternatives available.

Hypothesis 2

The effect of a stimulus change in one of the less frequently occurring alternatives upon the choice of the other alternatives is independent of the number of alternatives available.

Research plan

The subjects were homemakers from the Minneapolis area. They belonged to church associations which were compensated for their members' participation. There was a total of six church associations and each was divided in half for separate testing. Each half of an association served in a different test group. It was hoped that this would help to counterbalance any differences between church associations. Thus each test group contained approximately twenty-four homemakers, twelve from one church association and twelve from another church association.

For this investigation, cake mixes were chosen as the stimulus objects because of their familiarity and wide use by consumers. In addition, cake mixes are a well defined category of consumer goods containing many active competitors plus being a product of interest to the research sponsor.

Brand name was selected as the distinction between cake mixes because of the investigator's personal interest in brand names, and because of the belief that brand name is a product distinction which encompasses most consumer goods. However, other product distinctions such as flavor, color, etc., could have been selected instead of brand name.

Experimental design

In order to simplify the test design, only two sets of choice conditions were evaluated. The two-brand-choice condition was selected so that probability matching could be observed. Also, the five-brand-choice condition was chosen to observe the multiple-choice effect. This number of alternatives was selected after concluding that the optimum number of competing brands available to the consumer at the average retail outlet was five.

In the experimental design (see Table 4–3), the six test groups are divided into four experimental groups and two control groups. Experimental groups # 1 and # 2 had two brand choices and experimental groups # 3 and # 4 had five brand choices. All four experimental groups had price changes for Brand B after 300 trials.

Table 4–3. Experimental design

	Group	Choice conditions			
E	1	2 Brands	A = 39¢ B = 39¢	2 Brands	A = 39¢ B = 37¢
X	2	2 Brands	A = 39¢ B = 39¢	2 Brands	A = 39¢ B = 34¢
P					
E	3	5 Brands	A = 39¢ B = 39¢ C = 39¢ D = 39¢ E = 39¢	5 Brands	A = 39¢ B = 37¢ C = 39¢ D = 39¢ E = 39¢
R I M E					
N	4	5 Brands	A = 39¢ B = 39¢ C = 39¢ D = 39¢ E = 39¢	5 Brands	A = 39¢ B = 34¢ C = 39¢ D = 39¢ E = 39¢
T A L					
C	5	2 Brands	A = 39¢ B = 39¢	2 Brands	A = 39¢ B = 39¢
O N	6	5 Brands	A = 39¢ B = 39¢ C = 39¢ D = 39¢ E = 39¢	5 Brands	A = 39¢ B = 39¢ C = 39¢ D = 39¢ E = 39¢
T R O L					
		Trials 300		Trials 180	
		Total trials 480			

In experimental Groups 1 and 3 there was a 2 cent price drop in Brand B, while in experimental Groups 2 and 4 there was a 5 cent price drop in Brand B. The two control groups consisted of the two-brand condition and of the five-brand condition, with no price change in Brand B after 300 trials.

Procedure

The apparatus consisted of a 35 mm slide projector, slides, and screen. The subjects were seated at tables in front of the screen and given response

Table 4–4. Response sheet (two-choice condition)

	Brands			Brands	
1.	A	B	1.	B	A
2.	A	B	2.	B	A
3.	A	B	3.	B	A
4.	A	B	4.	B	A
5.	A	B	5.	B	A
6.	A	B	6.	B	A
7.	A	B	7.	B	A
8.	A	B	8.	B	A
9.	A	B	9.	B	A
10.	A	B	10.	B	A
11.	A	B	11.	B	A
12.	A	B	12.	B	A
13.	A	B	13.	B	A
14.	A	B	14.	B	A
15.	A	B	15.	B	A
16.	A	B	16.	B	A
17.	A	B	17.	B	A
18.	A	B	18.	B	A
19.	A	B	19.	B	A
20.	A	B	20.	B	A

(Version 1)   *(Version 2)*

Table 4-5. Response sheet (five-choice condition)

Brands						Brands					
1.	A	C	B	D	E	1.	A	C	B	D	E
2.	A	C	B	D	E	2.	A	C	B	D	E
3.	A	C	B	D	E	3.	A	C	B	D	E
4.	A	C	B	D	E	4.	A	C	B	D	E
5.	A	C	B	D	E	5.	A	C	B	D	E
6.	A	C	B	D	E	6.	A	C	B	D	E
7.	A	C	B	D	E	7.	A	C	B	D	E
8.	A	C	B	D	E	8.	A	C	B	D	E
9.	A	C	B	D	E	9.	A	C	B	D	E
10.	A	C	B	D	E	10.	A	C	B	D	E
11.	A	C	B	D	E	11.	A	C	B	D	E
12.	A	C	B	D	E	12.	A	C	B	D	E
13.	A	C	B	D	E	13.	A	C	B	D	E
14.	A	C	B	D	E	14.	A	C	B	D	E
15.	A	C	B	D	E	15.	A	C	B	D	E
16.	A	C	B	D	E	16.	A	C	B	D	E
17.	A	C	B	D	E	17.	A	C	B	D	E
18.	A	C	B	D	E	18.	A	C	B	D	E
19.	A	C	B	D	E	19.	A	C	B	D	E
20.	A	C	B	D	E	20.	A	C	B	D	E

sheets (Tables 4–4 and 4–5) and written instructions (Figure 4–1). Before beginning the session, a copy of the instructions was given each subject. The only difference in the instruction sheets for the brand-choice conditions was in the number of brands. The investigator then read the instructions aloud. Questions and clarifications were made by re-reading the appropriate part of the instructions.

The instructions were designed so the subjects did not receive information relating to how the "customer" might choose from among the brands. The purpose was to allow the subjects to make their initial selections based on their personal conceptions of the brands. Theoretically, the initial bases for selection would be altered in accordance with programmed choices as the trials continued.

The test began by the projection of the cake mixes (slides) on the screen. A slide of Brands A and B (two brands of white cake mix) or a slide of Brands A, B, C, D, and E (five brands of white cake mix) was projected on a screen in front of the subjects, depending upon the choice condition. For each of the test conditions, the subjects were presented with a total of 480 "show slides" and 480 "answer slides." (See Figures 4–2 and 4–3.) The "show slides" contained pictures of two or five brands of white cake mix, depending on the test condition. The subjects were shown a "show slide" and asked to make a prediction as to the brand of cake mix that was going to be purchased according to the situation presented in the instructions. After recording this prediction on her answer

---

The purpose of today's meeting is to see if you can predict the purchasing behavior of a group of shoppers. Recently, we placed five (two) white cake mixes on display in a local supermarket. Whenever a customer purchased one of the five (two) cake mixes the brand name was recorded by an observer. Thus, we know what brand was purchased by the first customer, what brand was purchased by the second customer, etc., for all of the customers who purchased a cake mix from this display.

We are interested in whether you can predict what brand the first customer purchased, what brand the second customer purchased, and so on for all of the cake mixes purchased from this display. You will do this by looking at a slide containing the five (two) white cake mixes with their prices just as the customer viewed them before making her purchase decision.

1. On your answer sheet you will notice that we have listed the five brands of cake mix in rows. The first row is marked 1 (left hand column) and this is where we would like you to make your prediction of what brand was purchased by the first customer. Please do this now by placing a circle around the brand you predict was purchased by the first customer. Remember that the slide shows the brands and their prices as the first customer saw them.
2. The next slide will be the same slide only with an arrow on the brand of cake mix that was actually purchased. If you made an incorrect prediction, please place a check ($\sqrt{}$) next to the brand that was actually purchased.
3. We will now go on to the next slide and make a prediction for the second customer in exactly the same manner.
4. There were approximately 500 customers who purchased cake mixes from this display, so you will be making 500 predictions for each of these 500 customers. You have already made predictions for the first two customers and saw whether your predictions were correct or incorrect. Remember, we are interested in how many correct predictions you can make, so be sure and observe the prices and the brands as did the customers actually making the purchase.

We will start out slowly and later speed up the slide changes as you get used to the routine.

Figure 4–1. Instructions to subjects.

Show slide

Answer slide

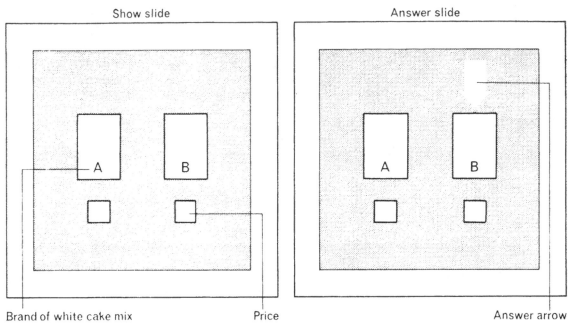

Brand of white cake mix   Price   Answer arrow

Figure 4–2. *Two-choice condition.*

Show slide

Answer slide

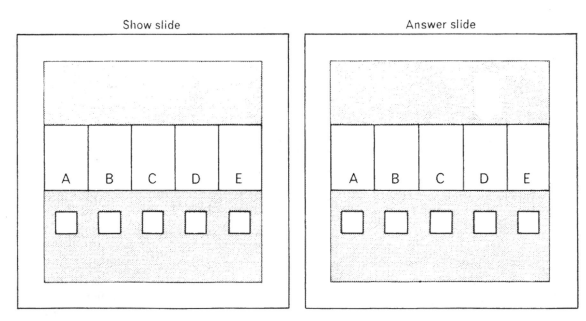

Figure 4–3. *Five-choice condition.*

sheet, the "answer slide" was shown indicating the correct brand purchased. This was graphically indicated by an arrow over the correct brand purchased. Thus, the "answer" and "show" slides were identical except for the arrow in the "answer slide."

A total of 960 slides were used for each test group. A Kodak Carrousel slide projector was used in the projection of the slides. With a total of 960 slides for each test group, 12 slide trays were required for each session.

A table of random numbers was used in constructing the programs for the two- and five-choice conditions. In the two-brand condition, Brand A randomly appeared correct 21 times in a block of 30 trials (70 per cent), while Brand B appeared correct nine times. In the five-brand condition, Brand A randomly appeared correct 21 times in a block of 30 trials (70 per cent), while Brands B, C, D and E each appeared correct two times with the extra correct choice randomly awarded to one of these four brands.

In order to counterbalance any response bias in the position of the brands in a slide, the various combinations of two and five brands were first determined. These combinations were then listed for the two- and five-choice conditions. The slide sequence for a programmed block of thirty slides was then constructed by referring to a table of random numbers.

Each subject observed the cake mixes and their prices before making a prediction as to which brand was purchased by the first customer. Next, the subjects were shown an identical slide except for an arrow over the brand that was purchased by the consumer. This sequence of a "show slide," prediction and "answer slide" represents one trial. There were 480 trials in each experimental and control group. A uniform pace of eight seconds per trial was maintained for all but the earliest trials. (The subjects were urged to make as many correct predictions as rapidly as possible.)

Also, they were instructed to make their own predictions and not to talk during the session. No mention was made of any possible price change in any of the brands. Thus, the price change was left to the subject's own visual detection.

The subjects made their predictions by circling the chosen brand on the response forms (Tables 4–4 and 4–5). If the subject made an incorrect prediction, that is, circled the brand that was not purchased, she corrected herself by placing a check (✓) next to the brand letters of the cake mix that was purchased. The response forms depended upon the choice condition. In the two-brand-choice condition, two versions were used (see Table 4–4). Version # 1 listed Brand A on the left and Brand B on the right. This was reversed in Version # 2. In the five-brand-choice condition, five versions were used. Here, Brand A was rotated in each of the five positions. The positions of the remaining four choices (B, C, D, and E) were randomly chosen in each of the five versions.

After the subjects had completed the first column of twenty predictions, the projector was stopped and the subjects were told that the projector would now be turned up to a four-second slide change. Whenever the subjects completed a page of predictions, the projector was stopped and a new carrousel of slides was attached. At the end of the seventh page, a short two-minute break was given the subjects.

Two sessions were conducted a day, one at 9:30 a.m. and one at 1:30 p.m.

The administration of the test took one hour and twenty minutes. Upon completion of the session, the subjects were allowed to ask questions and then were told the purpose of the study. No mention was made as to the identity of the research sponsor. Members of each session were asked not to disclose the mechanics or purpose of the session to any of their friends who may have been participating in the later sessions. The sessions were held in the respective association's church or in private homes.

See Problem 4–11 at the end of this chapter, pages 73 and 74.

Name   Instructor

Date   Section

Problem 4-1

Below are two experimental designs which might be used. For each design (1) give its name, (2) state what the experimental variable is, and (3) calculate the value requested (show your work):

A. A manufacturer of dried apricots feels his biggest problem is to get consumers acquainted with his product. An experiment is run in which 1,000 free samples of the dried apricots are distributed. This group and another group of 1,000 people to which free samples had not been given are both sent coupons for the purchase of dried apricots at a discount at grocery stores. The keyed coupons show that 480 coupons are returned from the group receiving the free sample and 400 are received from the other group. What is the effect of the experimental variable?

1. _____

2. _____

3. _____

B. The sale of Birds Eye cranberries in San Francisco for the month of March, 1969, is measured and gives a value of 55,000 units. An extensive TV advertising campaign is run during April and then the May sales are recorded. If it is established that the effect of the experimental variable is 12,000 units, what value was recorded for the May sales?

1. _____

2. _____

3. _____

Problem 4-2

A manufacturer of garden hose plans to add a small garden tool as a free gift for anyone purchasing a 100-foot garden hose in the month of June. He would like to evaluate the effect of such an approach on sales in a test market situation before deciding to use the approach nationally. His measurements will consist of retail sales in the test market.

1. State what the experimental variable is.

2. Select the experimental design which you feel is most applicable, briefly justifying your selection.

3. Construct a diagram for the suggested design to show for each group in the design what measurements are required and into which groups the experimental variable is introduced.

Name   Instructor

Date   Section

Problem 4-3

1. Suppose we are interested in changing the completely randomized design presented in illustration on page 52 to a randomized block design by restricting the random assignment of treatments, so that each treatment will appear once in each store. That is, we are interested in a randomized block design using stores as blocks with possible random assignment of treatments to stores. Show the design.

2. How would the randomized block design look if, instead of using stores as blocks, we are interested in using time periods as blocks with possible random assignment of treatments to time periods?

Problem 4-4

A retailer wants to combine several different existing package designs. Based on preliminary research, he finds that there are three basic designs suitable. Let us call these designs A, B, and C. The retailer wishes to test them in the market place to ascertain consumer acceptance. He has six stores available. He desires three weeks of testing (week 1, week 2, and week 3). Assume that all other promotional factors besides the three different package treatments will be held constant throughout the experiment. Set up a randomized block design for this experiment, showing the weeks, the stores, and the treatments they will receive.

Problem 4-5

Consider a taste-testing experiment of three blends of carbonated beverage. (These will be identified as A, B, and C.) Also assume that there are only three subjects available. Each subject will taste each blend. The objective is to control the order of tasting. It is decided that a Latin square is the most appropriate for such a testing. Show this experimental design below, clearly labeling the subjects, the order of tasting, and the three blends being tested.

Problem 4-6

An experimenter wants to determine the influence of various factors affecting readership of advertisements in magazines. He decides to place four different ads of the same size in four different magazines, in four different sections of the magazine, and in four positions on the page.

The rows will represent the positions on page. The columns will represent the four magazines. Within each cell, use capital letters A, B, C, and D to indicate sections of the magazine and use Greek letters (α, β, γ, and δ) to represent the four different types of advertisements. Set up a Latin square design for this experiment.

Problem 4-7

A company has sales outlets in several market areas, and its advertising is carried out locally in each of its market areas. Presently, its advertising budget in each market area is $1,000 per month.

The company's research director is interested in experimenting with different advertising budget levels to see how they affect sales response. For this purpose, he has decided on three budget levels (treatments): (A) $1,000 per month, (B) $2,000 per month; (C) $3,000 per month. He is interested in testing these three treatments (A, B, and C) in each area during three time periods (I, II, and III) in order to eliminate area differences. It is conceivable that the order of treatments will also affect results. Since there is a total of six possible sequences, a minimum of six areas are required for the experiment. Assume these six areas can be arranged into two groups of three areas each. Assume, further, that they are similar.

Denote the test areas by 1, 2, 3 and so on. Show the double change-over design.

Problem 4–8

A marketing research department is interested in evaluating the company's current promotional approach. Presently it is using a combination of media advertising and merchandising as its regular promotion program (A). It is interested in ascertaining how effective this program is compared with a cooperative advertising arrangement with retail (food) organizations wherein costs would be shared (B), and no advertising or promotion of any kind for their grocery product (C). To answer these questions, a controlled experiment utilizing the basic design for estimating carry-over effects is deemed most appropriate by the marketing research department. Four time periods of six weeks each are selected to give the firm ample opportunity to intensify and repeat its promotional efforts and also to permit the retailer ample opportunity to tie in his promotion activities with the firm's regular and cooperative advertising programs.

Six cities are selected, in which self-service food stores will be chosen for measuring sales during each treatment period. Three cities are in the northeast (Philadelphia, Syracuse, and Springfield, Mass.), and three are in the midwest (St. Louis, Omaha, Des Moines). The midwest is considered an area of heavy users of this product and the northeast is considered an area of light users.*

Set up a double change-over design for this problem.

*Based on Hoofnagle, *op. cit.*, p. 157.

Problem 4-9

A new soft drink is under study to find a formula with the most acceptable taste appeal. A factorial design allows measurement of two critical product variables—flavor intensity and sugar level—and determination of the most acceptable combination of levels. Sugar content is varied at four levels and flavor is also varied at four levels, yielding 16 product formulations (a, b, c, . . . p). Set up an experiment showing the two factors and their combinations.

Problem 4-10

We are interested in studying the effects of three factors: price, color of package design, and display levels. It is planned to vary price at 10¢, 13¢ and 16¢. Two package designs will be tested—blue and red. Two levels of display—high and low—will be used. Set up a factorial design ($3 \times 2 \times 2$) to show the factors, their variations, and their combinations.

Name	Instructor
Date	Section

Problem 4-11

Identify the ingredients of the experiment (as discussed in Chapters 2 and 3, and as indicated in Figure 2-1), for the "Customary prices" experiment (reproduced below). Mark in the margins the various factors (ingredients) by drawing arrows and identifying the components.

Customary prices

For many years, retail prices in this country have been quoted at one or two cents below the decimal unit—$.49, $.79, $.98, $1.49, $1.98, tell the tale. Several years ago, one of the large mail-order houses undertook an experiment to discover the significance of these customary prices. If they proved to be of no particular importance, substantial economies in accounting were in the offing. The merchandising executives suspected that the pricing tradition survived because of universal indulgence; they believed that, if attacked, it would soon give up the ghost. But this was only a suspicion; hence, they proceeded cautiously.

Excellent opportunities were afforded to control the experiment. The concern issued annually two large catalogues, in the Spring and in the Fall; also two small ones, known to the trade as flyers, aimed at stimulating trade during the dull months. Its principal competitor followed suit. The test was undertaken one Spring. The total edition of the catalogue numbered approximately 6,000,000. Variations in merchandise offered and featured—a recognition of economic and climatic differences—resulted in the production of regional catalogues. However, identity rather than dissimilarity was their outstanding characteristic. A group of representative items was selected and priced in several regional catalogues at $.50, $.80, $1, $1.50, $2; in the remainder of the edition these identical commodities were presented as customary prices: $.49, $.79, $.98, $1.49, $1.98.

The results of the experiment were as interesting as they were perplexing. For certain items, the change from the customary to the rounded price indicated that sales were halved; for others, no appreciable effect was noticeable; for still others, sales were disproportionately large. Throughout the trial the prices of the leading competitor had, of course, remained unchanged. Detailed records of sales in the preceding and present period by classes and by regions permitted the company to account, with a fair degree of certainty, for all variables influencing demand, other than the departure from customary prices. Although considerable effort was devoted to interpreting the results, the data would not lend themselves to generalizations. The vice-president in charge of merchandising ventured the guess that the losses were balanced by the gains. He realized full well that a repetition of the experiment might yield sufficient additional data to permit of more definite conclusions. But when a change of one cent a yard led to a loss of $50,000, the experimental zeal, even of a daring businessman, was likely to be held in check. Next time the losses might not be offset. One thing was clear: competition was itself a custom limited by the history of institutions, by the psychology of the competitors. The searcher after profits would continue to pay his respects to both.*

*Eli Ginzberg, "Customary Prices," *American Economic Review*, Vol. XXVI, No. 2 (1936), p. 296.

5

Experiments—from the laboratory to the field

Scholars and researchers in other disciplines have made contributions over a long period of time. Some of these contributions are the result of laboratory and others of field experimental research. Their successes with problems which are similar to some marketing problems cause us to be optimistic about the possibilities of advancing the experimental method in marketing.

There are reasons for the conviction that valuable, long needed insights into consumer behavior, for instance, may arise in the experimental laboratory and subsequently in the field. Those in the social sciences have developed experimental methods of identifying, controlling, and quantitatively measuring many of the important variables affecting individual and group motivation. Experimental methods with individuals have produced insights into the decision-making process beyond those previously garnered by other methods. Experiments with groups have yielded valuable information on factors such as leadership, reference groups, and effects of communications. Within the marketing profession itself there has been reported a number of well-conceived and well-conducted experiments. The experimental technique stands ready to take its place with other marketing research practices. As with any one of the other techniques, the experiment is not the answer to all marketing problems. Indeed, progress should come slowly and carefully in order to avoid some of the unfortunate misuses of previously introduced tools.[1]

Laboratory Experimentation

A laboratory experiment is a research study in which the variance of all or nearly all of the possible influential independent variables not pertinent to the immediate problem of the investigation is kept at a minimum. This is done by isolating the research in a physical situation apart from the routine of ordinary living and by manipulating one or more independent variables under rigorously specified, operationalized, and controlled conditions.[2]

Three elements are important in a laboratory experiment: (1) manipulation of independent variables, (2) setting up special conditions in which manipulation takes place, and (3) observation of dependent variables.

In a laboratory experiment the events of the experiment occur at the discretion of the experimenter. The observation process is started or stopped at the will of the experimenter. "The experimenter determines the treatments to which groups will be exposed, in what order, and at what time. In addition, the experimenter can select the points at which measurements will be taken, by what means, and on whom."[3]

Real-life situations are characterized by the operation of complex variables. In such a situation, it is difficult to determine the variables or to isolate the variables in order to study their interactions. There is no active control in the natural setting. However, the laboratory setting offers an opportunity for tight control which simplifies identification, elaboration, and verification of functional relationships between variables. The controlled situation and the manipulation of independent variables systematically increase the precision and repeatability of the experiment. . . .

The artificiality of laboratory experiments in marketing, as in other social sciences, does not diminish their usefulness as a tool of social research. However, caution must be exercised in

1. R. J. Holloway and T. White, "Advancing the Experimental Method in Marketing." Reprinted from *Journal of Marketing Research*, Vol. I (January, 1964), p. 25; published by the American Marketing Assoatation.

2. Fred N. Kerlinger, *Foundations of Behavioral Research* (New York: Holt, Rinehart and Winston, Inc.), 1966, p. 379.

3. K. E. Weick, "Laboratory Experimentation with Organizations," in J. G. March (editor), *Handbook of Organizations* (Chicago: Rand McNally, 1965), p. 199.

extending laboratory findings to the real-life marketing situation. Ideally, the findings of laboratory experiments should provide new hypotheses that would be tested in the field.

There is a dangerous temptation to generalize experimental findings beyond the laboratory. The marketing researcher who conducts a laboratory experiment and finds some relationship between variables should not forget that the relationships have yet to be tested in non-laboratory situations.[4]

Illustration: effects of alternatives on buying decisions

This study also examined the effect of the number of choices offered the consumer. It was reasoned that the amount of dissonance[5] was related to the number of alternatives offered. More specifically, the following two hypotheses were formulated:

1. The greater the number of relatively attractive alternatives, the more dissonance will be created after the choice decision; hence, the more pressure to reduce dissonance by re-evaluation of the chosen and rejected alternative(s).

2. The more equal the attractiveness of each dissimilar alternative and the greater the desirability of the alternatives, the more dissonance will be created after the choice decision; hence, the more pressure to reduce dissonance by re-evaluation of the chosen and rejected alternative(s).

In general, it was expected that if the individual was motivated to reduce dissonance after the choice decision was made, he would increase the desirability of the chosen alternative and decrease the desirability of the rejected alternative(s). This, in effect, would enhance the desirability of the chosen alternative relative to the position of the rejected alternative(s), thereby reducing the degree of post-decision dissonance.

Method

Subjects were chosen from several University classes during the summer session program. Each subject was assigned to one of the four experimental conditions on a random basis. In two instances, the subjects were reassigned because their pre-desirability scores did not fit the assigned condition.

4. M. Venkatesan, "Laboratory Methods in Marketing Research," in M. Venkatesan and Robert Mittelstaedt (editors), *Current Perspectives in Marketing Research* (New York: Free Press, Inc.), forthcoming.

5. See pages 56 – 57 for dissonance discussion.

Two alternatives	1. Both high in desirability*	2. One high and one low in desirability
Four alternatives	3. All high in desirability	4. One high and three low in desirability

*Desirability was determined from the first rating scale completed by the subject.

Sixteen products were used in the study. The order of presentation was randomized to avoid order bias.

tennis net	lantern
lady's pen	lady's watch
percolator	broiler
floor mat (car)	wax and polish kit
golf balls	fishing pole
pin and earrings	pearl necklace
toaster	portable beater
spotlight	seat belts

One subject entered the laboratory for each experiment. He was told that manufacturers frequently asked potential buyers for their evaluations of products. His evaluation for each product was sought on a separate rating scale, 0 (not at all desirable) to 8 (completely desirable). He was to evaluate the products according to his desire to buy at that time. In essence, which would he prefer to acquire now?

The ratings enabled the experimenter to select a *conflict* situation in which two or four articles rated high in desirability, or a *preference* situation in which both high and low ratings were given. The subject was then presented one of the four choice situations summarized above. The experimenter at this point told the subject he would be given one of these products if he would do four more hours of work in the laboratory.

Following the subject's decision, the experimenter discussed attributes of other products, attributes that might be useful in advertising the products. The subject was then asked to re-evaluate all 16 products, using the same type of rating. The subject was instructed to consider anew, much as he might if he had "slept on the problem all night." At this point the subject was told all about the experiment in the debriefing session. This experiment was conducted entirely in the laboratory. It was found that a thorough debriefing of each subject avoided any unpleasantness which might have occurred from the deception.[6]

See Problems 5–1 and 5–2 at the end of this chapter, pages 83 and 84.

6. Lee K. Anderson, James R. Taylor, and Robert J. Holloway, "The Consumer and His Alternatives: An Experimental Approach," *Journal of Marketing Research*, Vol. III (February, 1966), pp. 65–66.

Field experiments

The term "field experiment" refers to the environment in which an experiment is conducted. That is, a field experiment is conducted in a natural (i.e., not artificial) setting as contrasted with a laboratory experiment which is conducted in some especially arranged setting or environment. It is generally conducted out in the market place or, so to speak, "in the field." For example, a triangle type beer taste test conducted among randomly selected beer drinkers, brought into a brewery, would present an unnatural or special setting. By contrast, if the persons selected for the taste test received six packs of matched pairs for consumption in their homes—when they felt like it—the experiment would be more natural. This latter test could be considered a field experiment.

The difference between field and laboratory experiments is more one of degree than of form. The more natural or realistic the experimental setting, the more closely an experiment approaches a true field experiment. The more artificial or contrived the environment, the nearer an experiment is to the laboratory type. Fortunately, the ends on the continuum are clearly distinguishable from each other, even if intermediate positions are not.[7]

Strengths and weaknesses of field experiments

The control of the experimental field situation, however, is rarely as tight as the control of the laboratory experimental situation. We have here both a strength and a weakness. The investigator in a field study, though he has the power of manipulation, is always faced with the unpleasant possibility that his independent variables are contaminated by uncontrolled environmental variables. We stress this point because the necessity of controlling extraneous independent variables is particularly urgent in field experiments. . . .

One other weakness inherent in field experimental situations is lack of precision. In the laboratory experiment it is possible to achieve a high degree of precision or accuracy, so that laboratory measurement and control problems are usually simpler than those in field experiments. In realistic situations, there is always a great deal of systematic and random noise.[8]

Illustration: measuring commercials on CATV

During the past three years a unique methodology called Split-Cable has been developed using CATV (Community Antenna Television) systems to test television commercials. CATV systems employ electronically sensitive master antennas to receive distant, attenuated television signals. These signals are conveyed, via coaxial cable, to a headend or booster station. There special equipment boosts and modulates these signals to

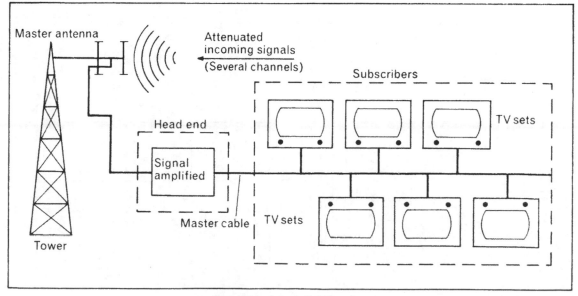

Figure 5–1. *A basic CATV system.*

7. Kenneth P. Uhl, "Field Experimentation: Some Problems, Pitfalls, and Perspective," in Raymond M. Haas (editor), *Science, Technology and Marketing.* Proceedings of the 1966 Fall Conference. (Chicago, Ill.: American Marketing Association), 1966, pp. 562–563.

8. Kerlinger, *op. cit.*, pp. 382, 383, 396.

appropriate strength and clarity for retransmission over a master cable line which branches out to the homes of the subscribers (see Figure 5–1).

How Split Cable operates

A CATV system using the Split Cable research method employs specially designed electronic gear at the headend which makes it possible to control television input absolutely by:

1. Blocking out any television commercials coming into the CATV system at any time on any channel, and
2. Simultaneously substituting a test commercial.

. . .

Test procedure

Although the cut-in period may be of any duration, our experience has indicated that a minimum of six weeks is usually required to obtain measurable differences. The exact pattern of commercial switching is, of course, determined by the research design, i.e., testing two alternative campaigns, 30-second versus 60-second commercials, etc.

The present Split Cable testing procedure utilizes interview waves both before and after the cut-in period, with the same respondents. The post-exposure interview is usually similar to, if not identical with, the pre-exposure interview, thus

pre- to post-changes can be compared between the sample groups. The measures employed fall into three main categories:

1. Attitudinal measures (rating scales, product image, product satisfaction, purchase intention),
2. Knowledge measures (awareness, level of knowledge, recall of slogans, copy points), and
3. Behavioral measures.

. . .

In addition to the special electronic blocking and substituting equipment, Split Cable also splits the one master cable line into a number of cable lines, each of which branches out to a specific section of the CATV system thus dividing the system into two (or more) samples (see Figure 5–2). It is thereby possible simultaneously to block out on-the-air television commercials of any duration, either uniformly or differentially, to either one or both sample groups, and replace them by test commercials. Table 5–1 shows how different treatments may be applied to the samples. These commercial cut-ins are conducted over specific time periods depending upon the requirements of the individual research designs.[9]

See Problems 5–3 and 5–4 at the end of this chapter, pages 85 and 86.

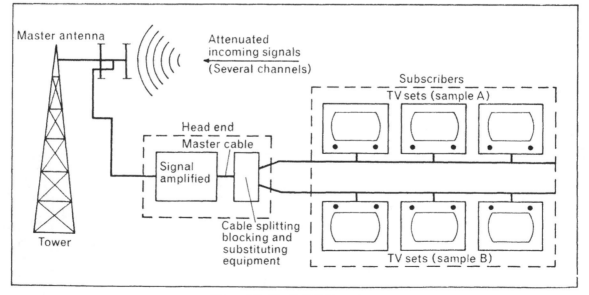

Figure 5–2. *The Split Cable system.*

9. E. Wallerstein, "Measuring Commercials on CATV," *Journal of Advertising Research*, Vol. 7 (June, 1967), pp. 15–19.

Table 5–1. Split Cable test procedures

Procedure	Sample A		Sample B	
1	On-the-air commercial		Test commercial	
2	Test commercial		On-the-air commercial	
3	Test commercial	1	Test commercial	1
4	Test commercial	1	Test commercial	2

Taking Procedure 4, the following occurs:

Time				
9:00:00 p.m.	Station ID		Station ID	
9:00:05 p.m.	Program X		Program X	
9:05:00 p.m.	Billboard		Billboard	
9:05:30 p.m.	Test commercial	1	Test commercial	2
9:06:30 p.m.	On-the-air commercial R		On-the-air commercial R	
9:07:30 p.m.	Program X		Program X	

The community split is planned to provide segments approximately equal in size and socioeconomic composition with a minimum of 1,000 households per segment. In addition, these segments are well matched on brand and product usage.

Simulation

The expense, time involved, or other problems associated with field experimentation may preclude it as source of information for a particular operational situation. In such cases it may be desirable to construct a model of the operational situation and "experiment" with it instead of the real-world situation. The manipulation of such models is called *simulation*.

This approach to obtaining information has a long history in, and is borrowed from, the physical sciences. An example of using physical analogs for simulative purposes is the use of scaled replicas of aircraft in a wind tunnel. The model can be tested under widely varying simulated conditions of attitude, altitude, and speeds, and its performance can be observed. It is far less expensive and time-consuming to use such simulation procedures than to construct and test actual prototype aircraft on test flights.

Physical analogs are not used in marketing, but conceptual models are constructed and manipulated to obtain information on the effect of varying combinations of the variables involved in specified ways. The information obtained consists of numerical outputs from the simulation models. As such, it differs from that provided by secondary sources, respondents, and field experimentation. These latter sources provide information directly from the situation being investigated. Simulation provides information from an imitation of this situation. Simulation in marketing uses a variety of procedures. *Monte Carlo techniques, operational gaming, experimental gaming,* and *heuristic programming* are classified as falling within the area of simulation methods. . . .

Another type of simulation which is gaining increasing attention is experimental gaming. . . .

Experimental gaming is distinguishable from business gaming in that the former technique is used primarily for research purposes rather than as an educational and training device. In experimental gaming the analyst may have formulated certain hypotheses about subject behavior. The complexity of the real world and the difficulty of control may militate against testing these hypotheses under ongoing conditions. The analyst may be able, however, to construct an artificial environment which mirrors some of the essentials of the real world and use this artificial environment as a laboratory in which to test various behavioral hypotheses.[10]

Illustration: a new way to determine buying decisions

If we raise the price of our brand, what share of the market are we likely to lose if competitors do not follow suit? Or, if we fail to follow a general price increase, what additional share of the market can we expect to obtain?

Of the buyers lost to competing brands what brands will they tend to buy? How resistant are the buyers of our brand and competing brands to switching to a new brand?

Effective answers to such questions would help to reduce the guesswork entering into management's decisions concerning price, product design, and promotional activities. So, a pilot study is carried out to see if useful answers could be obtained.

Therefore, it seemed desirable to use simple approximations of the market. Experiments were designed which permitted people to make simulated shopping trips. Their goal, as on a real shopping trip, was to maximize the satisfaction that could be obtained from a combination of merchandise and money.

Each participant was told how much money he had available to spend, the assortment of brands available in each class of goods for which he was "shopping," and the price of each item. The means by which he could maximize his satisfaction were defined by the funds and assortments available on each shopping visit. If he "bought" foolishly, he "acquired" a group of items and an amount of "change" from his purchase that gave him less than maximum satisfaction. Careful buying reduced the chances of making a poor choice and increased the reward of having made a wise choice.

After each experiment one "shopper," selected

10. Paul E. Green and Donald S. Tull, *Research for Marketing Decisions* (Englewood Cliffs, N.J.: Prentice-Hall, Inc.), 1966, pp. 113, 414–415.

on a random basis, was given the actual items and change called for by the selections made during one of his shopping trips. Emphasis on the price was somewhat exaggerated by listing the items and their prices in a manner that encouraged comparison. However, failure to pay off on every shopping trip tended to offset this bias. The procedure followed created a fairly close parallel to real shopping conditions.

Business-administration students at the State College of Washington were selected as subjects. The first step was to ask the 103 subjects which brands of toothpaste and cigarettes they customarily purchased for personal use.

The second step was to prepare "assortment sheets" which listed all the brands available at the student book store in the selected classifications, plus an additional item in each classification labeled "A New Brand." The regular prices at which these items could be purchased were also noted. The basic assortments used in the experiments were those that the student would have found at a point in time in a retail store in which he frequently shopped. To eliminate the positional bias of a brand on a sheet, a brand's position in a column was changed from sheet to sheet.

Three separate experiments were conducted: experiment X, experiment Y and experiment Z.

For the X experiment, the price of each subject's preferred brands was increased a different amount on each of ten successive shopping trips. Thus, he was faced with deciding whether he would continue to purchase his preferred brands, or whether he would switch to some other brands.

In the Y experiment, each subject faced the same condition with respect to his preferred brands; but he was given only one other item, "A New Brand," to which he could switch in each classification.

In the Z experiment, the price of each subject's preferred brands was held constant, but all other brands in a classification were reduced by varying amounts on each shopping trip.

When the three sets of ten assortment sheets had been prepared for each subject, the subjects were assembled in groups of about thirty-five. They were shown samples of the merchandise, told about the method of paying off on a shopping trip, given instructions for handling the sets of sheets, and then asked to make simulated shopping trips at normal shopping speed, checking items that would maximize the value to them of a "mix" of merchandise and money. At the conclusion of each experiment, one subject was selected at random to receive the merchandise and change called for by his decisions on one of his shopping trips."

Figures 5–3 and 5–4 show the comparisons of brand-switching patterns for individual brands of cigarettes and toothpaste.

Illustration: an experimental game
In a marketing research survey, one of the subjects is to determine the relative contributions made by each of several factors in determining consumer behavior. Usually, we approach the consumer with questions relating to a single factor only. A more realistic approach is to present questions involving several factors, since this is typically the case in actual marketing decisions made by the consumer. In cases where the number of factors is not too great, a useful approach to this problem is some variation of an experimental game. Where

Cigarettes				
Brand	Original price	Number preferring brand	Did not switch	Switched to
A	26¢	19		A B C D E F G
B	26¢	15	B	A C D F
All others	26¢	14		A B D F H I
9	Total	48	5 0 5 10 15 Number of buyers	

Figure 5–3. *Comparison of brand-switching patterns for individual brands of cigarettes.*

11. Edgar A. Pessemier, "A New Way to Determine Buying Decisions." Reprinted from *Journal of Marketing*, XXIV (October, 1959), pp. 41–43, 45; published by the American Marketing Association.

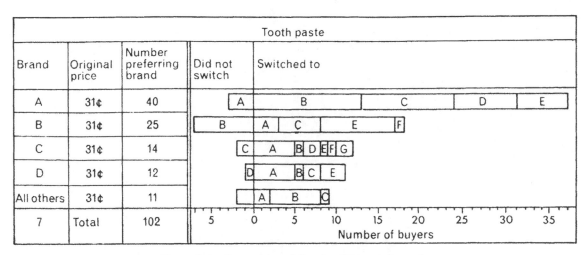

Figure 5–4. *Comparison of brand-switching patterns for individual brands of toothpaste.*

the number of factors is not too great, the consumer has an opportunity to consider each of them, and to make a choice or decision which, in some cases, seems to reflect decisions which are made in the market-place.

Let us consider the following hypothetical case.

Suppose that we are interested in the contributions made by *brand, store type,* and *distance* in the decision to purchase ice cream. We will suppose, further, that we are interested in each of these three factors at three levels.

> Factor One is *brand*; and we will suppose that the three brands are *Brand S, Brand B,* and *Brand A* ice cream.
>
> Factor Two is *store type*; and we will suppose that we are interested in a *candy store, drug store,* and *supermarket.*
>
> Factor Three is *distance*; and we will suppose that we are interested in what happens at distances of *one block, two blocks,* and *three blocks* from the home of the respondent.

We will now "mix" these factors to obtain all the possible combinations of them. Let us see what these combinations will be for one of our brands.

Alternative	Brand	Store type	Distance
A	Brand S	Candy store	1 Block
B	Brand S	Candy store	2 Blocks
C	Brand S	Candy store	3 Blocks
D	Brand S	Drug store	1 Block
E	Brand S	Drug store	2 Blocks
F	Brand S	Drug store	3 Blocks
G	Brand S	Supermarket	1 Block
H	Brand S	Supermarket	2 Blocks
I	Brand S	Supermarket	3 Blocks

Of course, we will be able to combine our factors for the other two brands (Brand B and Brand A) in the same nine ways, giving us a total of 27 alternatives. . . .

However, we will want to show each of our respondents three alternatives at a time to have her make a choice from among them. We might, for example, show her the following combination of alternatives:

For example:

1.	Brand S	Candy store	1 block
	Brand B	Drug store	2 blocks
	Brand A	Supermarket	3 blocks
2.	Brand S	Drug store	3 blocks
	Brand B	Supermarket	1 block
	Brand A	Candy store	2 blocks
3.	Brand S	Supermarket	2 blocks
	Brand B	Drug store	3 blocks
	Brand A	Candy store	1 block

There will be a total of 36 such combinations which can be made from our 27 alternatives.[12]

By getting the choices of each respondent to each of the conditions, it should be possible to ascertain 1-2-3 preferences among the choices.

See Problems 5–5 and 5–6 at the end of this chapter, pages 87 and 88.

12. A. J. Wood, "An Experimental Game," *Wood Chips,* Vol. 4 (November, 1959), pp. 1–8.

Name	Instructor
Date	Section

Problem 5–1

Using different products, set up an experiment which essentially is a replication* of the Anderson experiment on page 75. Follow his format, report the products used, experimental procedures followed, and measurements taken.

*Replication is the repetition of an experiment. Here it is used in the sense of "illustrative experiment," as described on page 2.

Problem 5-2

Refer to the experiment by Taylor (Number of alternatives and decision making) on page 57. Replicate his experiment by using two-brand-choice and three-brand-choice conditions. Use all male subjects and replicate the Taylor experiment with two brands of double-edged blades (or similar products used by male college students). Report below how you conducted this experiment and the results you have obtained.

Problem 5-3

Class Project: Consider the following examples of product evaluations:

In 1932, Laird conducted an experiment in which housewives were asked to examine and evaluate four pairs of silk stockings which were as identical as possible in manufacture, but differed in scent. The scents were so faint, however, that only six of the 250 housewives tested noticed them. Nevertheless, one pair of stockings (with a "narcissus" scent) was judged to be the best hosiery—on the basis of such attributes as texture, weave, feel, wearing qualities, lack of sheen, and weight—by 50% of the housewives. Another pair (with a "natural scent") was judged best by only 8%....

An experiment conducted by a large dairy found that consumers considered a cream colored, 14% butterfat ice cream to be richer in flavor than white colored, 16% butterfat ice cream.

Detergent manufacturers have found that housewives tend to judge the cleaning power of a detergent on the basis of suds level and smell. Similarly, the color of a detergent and its package is a cue often used to judge mildness. (Thus it is neither accident nor chemical necessity which leads manufacturers of liquid dish-washing detergents to color their products pink.)*

Set up a laboratory display of four pairs of nylon stockings. As described above, they should be identical in manufacture, and so on. Use three different scents, one on each pair; the fourth pair will not be scented. Obtain evaluation from female subjects on such attributes as texture, weave, feel, wearing qualities, sheen, and weight. What are the results? Write a report on the experiment and the results obtained.

*Donald F. Cox, "The Measurement of Information Value: A Study in Consumer Decision-Making," in William S. Decker (editor), *Emerging Concepts in Marketing*. Proceedings of the Winter Conference. (Chicago, Ill.: American Marketing Association), 1962, pp. 414–415.

Problem 5-4

Class Project: Refer to Cox's experiment on Responsiveness of food sales to supermarket shelf space changes (page 33). Replicate this experiment in a field setting if cooperation of a local retail food store can be obtained. Use two or three different grocery products as test products. Your instructor will suggest the type of products and the particular brands to be used. Explain how the replication was carried out.

Name	Instructor
Date	Section

Problem 5-5

Design a shopping simulation study which is for the purpose of determining the effect of prices ending in 9 versus 0. Assume a drug store situation, use men's toilet articles, and set it up in a small room equipped with shelves. A table could serve as the store counter. Write a report on how you designed and conducted the study.

Problem 5–6

Work up a shopping game which is a modification of Pessemier's study on page 79. Explain your shopping game in detail.

6

Analysis and presentation of results

Up to this chapter, our illustrations have been concerned with the methodology of experimentation. Experimentation, more than any other method, provides empirical evidence bearing on the hypotheses under investigation. Analysis of the data provided by the experiment is required to see whether the evidence is in accordance with the expectations of the investigator or fails to support the stated hypotheses.

Analysis is at the heart of the experimental method. The nature of experimental design and the type of measures, to some extent, predetermine the scope of analysis. As indicated by the dotted lines in Figure 6–1, the appropriate methods of analysis

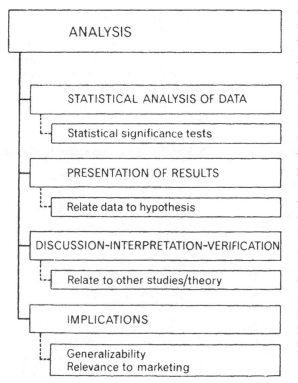

Figure 6–1. *A diagram of the analysis process.*

are planned very early in the research, long before the data are collected. No experimental inquiry should be planned without anticipating what will be done when the data have been collected or without considering the interpretation of the findings.

As Figure 6–1 illustrates, the analysis process of experimental results consists of (1) statistical analysis of data, (2) presentation of results, (3) discussion (including interpretation and verification), (4) implications. Generally, these four components are called "analysis and interpretation."

The first aspect of analysis is concerned with the existence or nonexistence of relationships between the variables under investigation. Contrary to other methods, experimental results are always analyzed with the appropriate statistical techniques to ascertain the relationships within the research design. In this sense, analysis and statistical interpretation of results are very closely interwoven. When you conduct an experiment and obtain results, it is conventional to statistically analyze the results to determine relationships.[1] Such statistically analyzed results are presented in the forms of tables and graphs; statistical significance is also indicated along with the results. All the evidence relevant to the research hypotheses and the statistical findings are reported, whether or not they support the hypotheses. Even negative results can be of great importance since they are useful in formulating new hypotheses, clarifying variables, and shaping future experiments. Generally only the tables most relevant to the hypotheses are presented.

---

1. It is assumed that our readers have the basic background in statistical inference tests.

In addition to the mechanical side of the analysis process, there is another aspect: the interpretation or discussion of the results. Bare statements of findings are not enough; nor does the existence of any relationship in and of itself provide any clear understanding of the phenomena under investigation. This aspect of analysis seeks the meaning and implications of the results. It tries to relate the results to findings from other studies and experiments. It seeks to compare the results of one's investigation with the findings of other researchers and with expectations derived from theories. In marketing, there are relatively few theories, but a considerable amount of theory is being brought in from a variety of disciplines. Interpretation usually determines whether the same results could be explained by plausible hypotheses other than the ones that have been formulated in the study. Interpretation is also concerned with the validity of the tested hypotheses and the reliability of the measures and procedures employed in the experiment. The following suggestion by the American Psychological Association regarding results and discussion is also applicable to researchers engaged in marketing experiments and in reporting their findings:

Discussion

The discussion should point out the limitations of the conclusions, note correspondence or differences between the findings and widely accepted points of view, and briefly give the implications for theory or practice.

Reports of research resulting in negative or unexpected findings should not end with long discussions of possible reasons for the outcome. Brief discussion is appropriate.[2]

The analysis process is difficult without an understanding of the nature of statistical inference and an appreciation for the cumulative nature of experimental findings. Students are strongly urged to develop an adequate background in statistical inference techniques. One writer has presented

2. *Publication Manual of the American Psychological Association* (Washington, D.C.), 1957, p. 11. Copyright 1957 by the American Psychological Association, and reproduced by permission.

the following guide for the analysis of experiments:

A guide for the analysis of experiment

I. What is the relationship between the marketing decision under consideration and the research design used in the investigation?

A. In terms of variables considered:

1. What variables are apt to be important determinants of the decision?
2. Of these, which are included in the research design?
3. What would you expect the effect to be of modifying the design so as to include more of the important determinants of the decision?
4. If such a modification is desirable from the standpoint of the problem, is it feasible in terms of its cost and the complexity of the research design?

B. In terms of the physical context of the research:

1. Was the experiment performed in the field or the laboratory?

   (a) If it was performed in the laboratory:
   (i) What were the laboratory conditions?
   (ii) How were these different from those under which the policies being evaluated will be implemented? (That is, is the motivation of the respondent apt to be the same in the laboratory as in the field?)
   (iii) In what way would you expect the observed results to change if some of these conditions were modified?
   (iv) Could the existing study be modified so as to bring the nature of the laboratory situation closer to that of the "real" world?
   (v) If the answer to the previous question was yes, why do you think these modifications were not made when the design was originally implemented?

   (b) If it was performed in the field: ask questions (a) i to (a) v.

2. Was the group of experimental units (individuals, stores, cities, and so on) apt to reflect the characteristics of the

population to be affected by the decision? If not:

(a) What are the differences apt to be between the population being investigated and the one that is being acted upon by the decision maker?

(b) If the population being investigated were modified so as to bring it closer to reflecting the characteristics of the population to be acted upon, in what way would you expect the results of the investigation to change?

(c) What modifications would you make? Why?

II. What is the nature of the experimental design under investigation?

A. How were the control groups organized?

1. Were before and after measurements taken?

(a) Was there apt to be any interaction between the before measurement and the experimental variable? Between the before and after measurement?

(b) If the answer to either of the questions on interaction is yes, then in what ways were the control groups organized to avoid these interactions?

(c) Could some other procedure be used?

2. Prior to the administration of the treatments, what was done to insure the comparability of the groups of units to be exposed to each treatment?

(a) In what ways could these procedures be modified so as to improve one's basis for comparison?

(b) What are the costs (money, time, and complexity) involved in the modifications? Do you think they are justified?

3. Was any supplementary data collected during the administration of the treatments in order to facilitate their comparison when the results were analyzed?

(a) What other supplementary information might have been desirable to collect?

(b) What would you do with the information if you had it?

(c) How would you expect it to modify the results?

B. Was randomization employed in the process of assigning treatments to experimental units? Why or why not, as the case may be?

C. In what fashion was the experimental response measured? Would some alternative unit of measurement be apt to yield more clear-cut results?

D. In cases where supplementary information was collected, what units of measurement were used with respect to each variable?

1. Were these operational definitions appropriate for the problem at hand?

2. How could they be modified so as to be more useful in terms of coming closer to a better measure of the variables under investigation in the experiment?

III. What are the implications of the analysis of this experiment with respect to possible applications to other marketing problems or to other product categories?

A. What were the characteristics of the product and/or the problem under investigation?

B. In what way do these characteristics differ with respect to other products and/or problems?

C. How are these differences apt to affect the potential contribution of experimentation to the solution of the problem? Or, to put it another way, with respect to what types of problems and/or product categories is experimentation apt to generate its most fruitful results in terms of its contribution to the evaluation of alternative management policies?[3]

Format of presentation

One of the goals of scientific research is the dissemination of its findings to scholars and researchers in the area. Since marketing experimentation is in its infancy, there is a great need to communicate the nature of these investigations, their empirical findings, and their implications for marketing

3. Reprinted with permission from Ronald E. Frank, Alfred A. Kuehn, and William F. Massey, *Quantitative Techniques in Marketing Analysis* (Homewood, Ill.: Richard D. Irwin, Inc.), 1962, pp. 52–54.

researchers in general and for marketing practitioners in particular. Findings of experimental research have now become fairly standard in both the physical and the social sciences. Examine an issue of the *Journal of Marketing Research* to see how the experimental findings are presented. Generally, the divisions of such articles are: Title, Introduction, Method, Results, Discussion, Implications, and, sometimes, Conclusions or Summary. The components in the presentation of experimental research are outlined in Figure 6–2.

Figure 6–2. *A suggested outline.*

Title

1.0 *Abstract* (120 words or less)

2.0 *Introduction*
   2.1 Literature survey (summary)
   2.2 Exposition of problem
   2.3 Statement of hypotheses
   2.4 Definitions

3.0 *Method*
   3.1 Design of the experiment (research plan)
   3.2 Subjects utilized
   3.3 Instruments and techniques of measurement (including the description of any apparatus used)
   3.4 Experimental procedure (how the experiment was conducted)
      3.41 Manipulation and control techniques
      3.42 How variables were measured
   3.5 Pilot study results (if relevant)

4.0 *Results and discussion*
   4.1 Summary of results (in tabular form—including statistical significance)
   4.2 Interpretation of results
   4.3 Relevance to and verification of other studies and theories
   4.4 Suggested further research (including advancement of new hypotheses)

5.0 *Implications*
   5.1 Generalizability
   5.2 Relevance to marketing

6.0 *Conclusions* (if needed)
   References

Illustration of analysis and presentation of results

The published report of an experiment by Cardozo is reproduced in its entirety on the following pages so that you may become familiar with the analysis process and also with the format of presentation of experimental results.

An experimental study of customer effort, expectation, and satisfaction*

RICHARD N. CARDOZO

Results of a laboratory experiment indicate that customer satisfaction with a product is influenced by the effort expended to acquire the product, and the expectations concerning the product. Specifically, the experiment suggests that satisfaction with the product may be higher when customers expend considerable effort to obtain the product than when they use only modest effort. This finding is opposed to usual notions of marketing efficiency and customer convenience. The research also suggests that customer satisfaction is lower when the product does not come up to expectations than when the product meets expectations.

Customer satisfaction with a product presumably leads to repeat purchases, acceptance of other products in the same product line, and favorable word-of-mouth publicity. If this assumption is correct, then knowledge about factors affecting customer satisfaction is essential to marketers [3].

Knowledge about customer effort and expectation is important because these factors are major components of customer behavior, and because management can, within limits, influence the amount of effort customers expend and their expectations. Customer effort includes the physical, mental, and financial resouces expended to obtain a product. One way to alter the amount of effort customers expend is to make the purchase decision more or less difficult by varying the amount of information supplied to the customer. If very little information is supplied, the customer may have to expend effort to gather additional information; if a great deal of detailed information is supplied, the customer may have to expend considerable effort to process the information. The expectations customers have regarding a product depend upon information gathered from a variety of sources. Within limits, customer expectations may be influenced by advertising, or other sales promotion methods.

Research plan

Since the literature of marketing and eco-

nomics provided neither exact definitions nor rigorous discussions of customer effort and expectation, it was felt that a fairly precise investigation of these factors might be useful. This precision could be obtained, however, only by severely limiting the range and scope of the investigation. Several considerations pointed to the use of a laboratory experiment for such a study:

1. Controlled laboratory experiments had been successfully employed in other fields for limited investigations.

2. A laboratory setting would permit study of the factors in relatively pure form, and such study might provide useful analytical information despite its limited nature, and would provide a basis for further research.

3. A laboratory experiment would allow maximum utilization of psychological theory, itself based upon laboratory findings.

In fact, two branches of psychological theory ("contrast" theory and "dissonance" theory) provided the basis for making specific statements about the relationships among effort, expectation, and evaluation. Contrast theory implies that a customer who receives a product less valuable than he expected will magnify the difference between the product received and the product expected. Even if this original expectation were to change, he would still be free to compare unfavorably the product received with better ones [5]. For example, suppose a customer goes to a restaurant which he expects to be good, and is confronted with an unappetizing meal. He might say that the restaurant was one of the worst he had ever been in and that the food

*Reprinted, with permission, from *Journal of Marketing Research*, Vol. II (August, 1965), pp. 244-249.

was unfit for human consumption, *etc*.

A study by Spector [6] supports this argument. Spector found that subjects whose expectations were negatively disconfirmed evaluated a reward less favorably than did subjects who expected and received the same reward. In other words, disappointed subjects magnified the difference between the presumably more desirable reward and the one they received.

On the other hand, Festinger's theory of cognitive dissonance [4] might lead one to predict the opposite effect. Dissonance theory would imply that a person who expected a high-value product and received a low-value product would recognize the disparity and experience cognitive dissonance. (Dissonance is aroused in this case because receiving a low-value product is not consistent with having expected a high-value product.) The existence of dissonance should produce pressures for its reduction, which could be accomplished by adjusting the perceived disparity. One possible method to reconcile the difference between expectation and product would be to raise the evaluation of the product received.

In terms of the restaurant situation, the customer might say that the food was not really as bad as it appeared, that he really liked overcooked meat, *etc*. The work of Brehm [1] and Brehm and Cohen [2] indicates that people may raise their evaluations of those products which they have chosen from an array of products, when the cost to the individual of the chosen product is high.

Some reconciliation of the conflicting predictions made by contrast theory and dissonance theory is possible by introducing the concept of effort. If an individual expends effort in a situation, it is likely that the outcome of the experience has some importance for him. For instance, if our diner had made elaborate plans, driven a long distance, and paid a high price for his meal, he would probably have been much more concerned about enjoying his meal than a person who had merely stopped by the restaurant because it was convenient. Even if the outcome of this dining experience had not had initial importance, the investment of effort would have led our diner to attribute it importance.

Thus, when a customer expends considerable effort, the prediction from dissonance theory might be expected to hold, since the consequences of that situation are important to the customer. However, when little effort is expended, the result predicted by contrast theory might be expected to occur since the outcome of the situation is not so important. In other words, when a customer has expended little effort and receives a product less valuable than expected, he might evaluate that product less favorably than would a customer who expected, and did obtain, the identical product. However, as a customer expends greater effort, the situation becomes more important, and some dissonance is aroused when disappointed. Dissonance may be reduced by decreasing the perceived disparity between expectation and reward, but it cannot be reduced by magnifying the disparity. Thus, under conditions of high effort, dissonance reduction processes would tend to decrease the differences in product evaluation between customers who were disappointed and those who were not.

The expenditure of effort itself may produce a perceived disparity between effort expended and product received, whether customers obtained what they expected or less than they expected. If customers who expend little effort receive a product they consider appropriate for that amount of effort, those who invest considerable effort and obtain the same product are likely to perceive a disparity between effort and reward. Since magnifying this disparity would increase the dissonance aroused in this situation, customers are not likely to contrast effort and reward. Rather, they are likely to raise their evaluations of the product (or to deny the effort) relative to customers who have expended little effort to obtain the same product. This analysis presumes that the disparity is not so great that the individual withdraws from the situation altogether.

The reasoning expressed above leads to the following hypotheses, which were evaluated in a laboratory setting.

HYPOTHESES

1. When customers expend little effort to obtain a product, those who receive a product less valuable than they expected will rate that product lower than will those who expected to receive, and do receive, the same product.

2. As effort expended increases, this effect decreases.

3. When customers obtain a product less valuable than they expected, those who expended high effort to obtain the product will rate it higher than will those who expended little effort.

4. When customers obtain a product about as valuable as they expected, those who expended high effort to obtain the product will rate it higher than will those who expended little effort.

Procedure

The hypotheses were evaluated in a catalog shopping situation. Each of the independent variables, effort and expectation, appeared at two levels. The design was a two-by-two factorial, as shown in the following tabulation:

Effort (F)	Expectation (X)	
	Low (l)	High (h)
Low (l)	A	B
High (h)	C	D

Subjects were 107 college juniors and seniors in the School of Business Administration, University of Minnesota.

Expectation was manipulated by the use of two 31-item catalogs in the study. Both contained descriptions and prices of ball-point pens of the type usually purchased by the subjects. The high expectation catalog contained products whose median price was about $1.95. The products shown in the low expectation catalog where priced between 29¢ and 59¢; the average price was about 39¢. All subjects received the same 39¢ pen, ostensibly chosen by lot from the samples provided by the manufacturers whose products were shown in the catalog. Thus, the rational expectation of a student who saw the high expectation catalog was a $1.95 writing instrument; of a student who used the low expectation catalog, a 39¢ pen.

Effort was manipulated by a simulated shopping task. The task required low effort subjects to look through one of the catalogs as if shopping, and to write down one feature which impressed them for half of the items shown. This minimum effort procedure took about 15 minutes. High effort subjects worked about an hour in uncomfortable surroundings. They were asked to comb one catalog carefully, and to record five different features about each of the 31 items. The purpose of their task was to force them to invest considerable shopping effort.

The dependent measure was a questionnaire on which the product and shopping situation were rated, each on several scales. Subjects evaluated both the pen they received and the simulated shopping experience immediately after receiving the product. Subjects indicated their evaluations by placing an "X" along each of several 100 millimeter lines. For example, an individual who felt that the product he received was about the same as others in the catalog might have placed an X in the middle of the line shown below:

Compared to the products shown in the catalog, this product is:

Very inferior	Rather inferior	Somewhat superior	Vastly superior
(0)		X	(100)

Questionnaires were scored by measuring the distance in millimeters from the zero end of the line to the point where the X crossed the line.

Results and discussion

The results† of the experiment indicated that effort and expectation did influence evaluation of the product. Table 6-1 shows an index of product evaluation, based on an unweighted combination of responses on

---

†The results presented are based on data from 88 of the 107 students who participated. The remaining 19 were suspicious of the procedure. Excluding data from these 19 subjects slightly altered the size of some of the differences among treatment combinations, but did not affect the direction of any differences.

the "product desirability" and "comparison-to-catalog" questions. Responses on the remaining four product evaluation questions (product usefulness, price, comparative quality, comparative value), and indexes based on them, yielded substantially the same results as those presented in the table. In some cases the differences among treatment combinations were more dramatic; in others, they were less so.

Table 6–1. Index of mean product evaluation scores*

Effort (F)	Expectation (X)	
	Low (l)	High (h)
Low (l)	51	35
High (h)	54	44

Comparisons among scores		
Individual treatment combinations		Level of significance
Low effort:	$X_l - X_h = 16$	.01
High effort:	$X_l - X_h = 10$	.05
Low expectation:	$F_h - F_l = 3$	.20
High expectation:	$F_h - F_l = 9$	.05

Main effects and interaction		
Expectation treatments combined:		
$F_h - F_l = 6$		.05
Effort treatments combined:		
$X_l - X_h = 13$		.01
Interaction		
$(X_l - X_h)F_l - (X_l - X_h)F_h = 6$		.05

* Maximum score = 100.

HYPOTHESIS 1

The results supported the first hypothesis: when subjects expended little effort, those who received a product less valuable than they expected rated it much less favorably than did subjects who expected to receive, and did receive, the identical product. The same result occurred within the high effort treatment: subjects who received less than they expected rated the product less favorably than did those who received about what they expected. When the effort treatments were combined, the same phenomenon was observed—subjects who shopped the high expectation catalog and received the low-priced pen rated it less favorably than did subjects who shopped the low expectation catalog and received the identical low-priced pen.

If the experimental procedure succeeded in creating, and then confirming or discon-

firming expectations, one may say that the effect of negative disconfirmation of expectation was to produce a *less favorable* evaluation of the product. Even if the procedure employed did not create firm expectations, it may be said that the perceived disparity between the product received and the products in the high expectation catalog apparently operated to produce a less favorable evaluation of the product received. In any event, it appears that the catalogs provided standards for the evaluation of the product subjects received.

HYPOTHESIS 2

The results supported Hypothesis Two: as effort increased, the difference between high and low expectation subjects' ratings of the product would decrease. Specifically, the hypothesis predicted a difference between differences, or an interaction:

$$(X_l - X_h)F_l > (X_l - X_h)F_h$$

Table 6–2 shows that product evaluations were only slightly higher in the high effort, low expectation condition than they were in the low effort, low expectation condition. On the other hand, evaluation scores in the high effort, high expectation condition (while lower than those in the high effort, low expectation condition) were considerably higher than those in the low effort, high expectation condition. These observations indicated that expenditure of greater effort moderated the effect of negative disconfirmation of expectation. In order to understand this phenomenon, it may be useful to analyze each of the high expectation conditions in greater detail.

In the low effort, high expectation condition, subjects invested little time and energy, and had only limited knowledge on which to base their expectations. Consequently, the outcome of the experiment mattered little to them, and it was relatively easy to deny that they had expected a product more valuable than that received. Subjects in this condition were quite free to contrast the product unfavorably with those in the catalog, and to rate it as relatively undesirable.

In terms of dissonance theory, one may say that little dissonance would have been aroused in this condition, because the modest investment of effort minimized individual commitment to, or involvement in, the situation. Any dissonance which might have been aroused by the disparity between expecting a high value product and receiving a low value one could have been reduced by denying the expectation. Such denial would also have reduced any dissonance aroused by the disparity between expecting a valuable product and expending little effort.

On the other hand, subjects in the high effort, high expectation treatment had invested considerable time and energy before obtaining the product. This investment made the outcome of the experiment important to them, and provided substantial basis for firm expectations of receiving a high value product. In this situation, the disparity between expectation of a high value product and receipt of a low value product aroused some dissonance, which could have been reduced only by lowering or denying the rather firm expectation, or by raising the evaluation of the product. An unfavorable evaluation of the product could only have increased dissonance, whereas a more favorable evaluation of the product would have operated to reduce it.

A favorable evaluation would also have been consistent with subjects' knowledge that they had expended considerable effort to obtain the product: "If I've had to work to get it, the product must be pretty good." However, evaluation scores in this condition could not exceed the midpoint of any scale unless subjects felt that the 39¢ pen they received was superior to the $1.95 products in the high expectation catalog. Thus the "dissonance reduction" processes operating to produce a favorable rating could not entirely overcome the perceived disparity between the products in the catalog and the product received.

In summary: subjects in the low effort, high expectation condition had no reason to reduce the disparity between the expensive products they saw in the catalog and the inexpensive product they received; in fact, they were free to magnify the disparity. The result of their contrasting the product received with those in the catalog was to produce a much lower evaluation of the product in the low effort, high expectation condition than in the low effort, low expectation condition (where the product received was similar to those in the catalog).

Table 6–2. Typical shopping task evaluation scale and scores: mean scores on "pleasant" scale*

Effort (F)	Expectation (X)	
	Low (l)	High (h)
Low (l)	59	54
High (h)	43	49

Comparisons among scores

Individual treatment combinations		Level of significance
Low effort:	$X_l - X_h = 5$	.10
High effort:	$X_h - X_l = 6$	.10
Low expectation:	$F_l - F_h = 16$	.10
High expectation:	$F_l - F_h = 5$	.10

Main effects and interaction

Expectation treatments combined:		
$F_l - F_h = 11$		.01
Effort treatments combined:		
$F_h - F_l = 1$		.50
Interaction		
$(X_l - X_h)F_l - (X_l - X_h)F_h = 11$		.01

*The task itself was

Very pleasant (100)	Rather pleasant	Rather unpleasant	Extremely unpleasant (0)

In the high effort, high expectation condition, this contrast phenomenon was partially blocked. As a result, higher product evaluation scores were obtained in the high effort, high expectation condition than in the low effort, high expectation condition. But, because some disparity was still perceived between products in the catalog and the product received, product evaluation scores in the high effort, high expectation condition remained somewhat lower than those in the high effort, low expectation condition.

HYPOTHESIS 3

The results supported Hypothesis Three which asserted that, within the high expectation treatment, subjects who expended considerable effort would rate the product more favorably than would those who had put forth little effort. As discussed previously, evaluations of the product were lower in the low effort, high expectation condition than in the high effort, high expectation condition because contrast processes (leading to lower evaluations) were free to operate in the former condition, but were partially blocked in the latter.

HYPOTHESIS 4

The results were in the direction predicted by Hypothesis Four, but they were not statistically significant ($p = .20$, t-test). One reason for this small difference observed between high and low effort conditions within the low expectation treatment may have been that most subjects found it difficult to rate the product received higher than 60 on any scale. Consequently, the mean rating of 54 in the high effort, low expectation condition may approach the upper limit of the range within which subjects felt the product could reasonably be evaluated. This upper limit on evaluation may have prevented individuals from adjusting completely the disparity perceived between expending considerable effort and receiving an inexpensive product.

When expectation treatments were combined, the results showed that subjects in the high effort treatments evaluated the product more favorably than did those in the low effort treatments. The investment of greater effort apparently produced a more favorable evaluation of the product.

The expenditure of high effort provided subjects both more information and a greater opportunity for commitment than did the low effort treatment. In order to see whether subjects evaluated the product differently simply because they knew more about disposable ball-point pens, the following procedure was employed. Treatment combinations were ranked according to (1) number of products similar to the one received to which subjects were exposed in each catalog, and (2) number of product features of similar products which subjects had to record. Each of these rankings was compared to rankings of treatment combinations on both mean and median evalua-

tions of the product. The comparison was made for the "product evaluation" scale group as a whole, as well as for each scale within the group.

Correlations between each of the rank-orders mentioned did not differ significantly from zero. Although the data do not permit the inference that an "information hypothesis" may be rejected, it does appear that an explanation of the data in terms of effort and expectation may be more fruitful. The latter explanation does. for example, account for the observed interaction, which an information hypothesis would not have predicted.

An interesting sidelight to the analysis of the effect of information is that those subjects who recorded five features for each of 31 products (high effort) rated the products in the catalogs as "less clearly described" than did those who recorded only one feature for each of 16 products ($p < .05$, t-test). It may be that exposure to too much information makes discrimination among products *more*, rather than less, difficult.

EVALUATION OF THE SHOPPING TASK

Not surprisingly, subjects in the high effort treatments found the task less pleasant, more fatiguing and more frustrating, than did subjects in the low effort treatments. Within each effort treatment, however, some interesting reversals appeared. Within the low effort treatment, high expectation subjects found the shopping task significantly less pleasant and less rewarding than did low expectation subjects. The reverse was true within the high effort treatment, where high expectation subjects rated the shopping task more favorably than did low expectation subjects.

These results may be seen more clearly by examining a scale typical of those on which the shopping task was evaluated. Of the 12 scales, all but three showed differences in the same directions as those on the "pleasant" scale. For all three scales on which the direction was different from that shown on the pleasant scale, differences were well within the range of sampling error.

It appears that subjects in the low effort, high expectation condition generalized their unfavorable rating of the product to the shopping experience. On the other hand, subjects in the high effort, high expectation condition found some extra rewards in the shopping experience, compared to those in the high effort, low expectation condition.

This phenomenon may be interpreted from the point of view of dissonance theory. Subjects in the low effort, high expectation treatment were free to generalize their unfavorable reactions from the product to the shopping situation, for no dissonance was introduced by so doing. On the other hand, revaluating the shopping task in a more favorable light worked in the direction of reducing dissonance for subjects in the high effort, high expectation condition. They could narrow the perceived disparity between high effort and expectation, on the one hand, and low reward, on the other hand, by finding supplementary rewards in the shopping task.

Implications for marketing

The results of this experiment showed that, under certain conditions, effort and expectation affected the evaluation of both a product and a shopping experience. When expectations were negatively disconfirmed, subjects rated both product and shopping experience unfavorably. The expenditure of high effort moderated that effect and, for the shopping experience, partially reversed it. It is obvious that one should think twice about what we can assert from results obtained under limited conditions. Nevertheless, the results lead to some interesting implications for marketing.

EFFORT

Expenditure of higher effort produced a more favorable initial evaluation of the product. Thus, a simple notion of "efficiency" cannot prevail. The effort invested in shopping may, under specifiable conditions, contribute to the evaluation of the product. Although consumers often expend more effort to obtain products they value,

expenditure of high effort follows favorable evaluation in such cases. This experiment shows that a favorable evaluation may indeed follow the expenditure of high effort.

If a more favorable evaluation of a product is assumed to lead to a higher probability of repeat purchasing, one is led to the rather surprising conclusion that, within limits, greater shopping effort may lead to more repeat purchases. Although the logic of such an assertion is not unassailable, it does suggest that the notion of convenience (lack of effort) ought to be reexamined.

EXPECTATION

Under certain conditions, subjects used their expectations as guidelines against which they evaluated the product. Either their expectations, or an array of products with which they have had previous experience, may form such guidelines. What is new in the findings of this experiment is that failure of a product to measure up to these guidelines may result in no initial sale, no repeat sale, and possibly unfavorable word-of-mouth publicity. Such reactions should be expected particularly when little shopping effort has been invested.

If this interpretation is correct, marketers should endeavor to make their offerings consistent with customer guidelines, or standards. One way of achieving this goal is to manipulate expectations through sales promotion. An important corollary is that marketers should know what customer standards of evaluation are, and act accordingly.

SATISFACTION

Since both effort and confirmation or disconfirmation of expectation affect evaluation, customer satisfaction may depend not only upon the product itself, but also upon the experience surrounding acquisition of the product. Customer satisfaction, then, may be more a global concept than simply product evaluation. Satisfaction may involve evaluation of an entire product bundle or offering.

Since the shopping experience and the product are, under some conditions, evaluated differently, the definition and measurement of total satisfaction pose a complex problem. Besides evaluation of the product and shopping experience as described here, there may be still other elements of satisfaction which have not been identified, and whose impact remains to be examined.

REFERENCES

1. BREHM, JACK W. "Postdecision Changes in the Desirability of Alternatives," *Journal of Abnormal and Social Psychology*, Vol. 52 (1956), pp. 384–389.

2. ———, and COHEN, ARTHUR R. *Explorations in Cognitive Dissonance* (New York: John Wiley & Sons, Inc.), 1962.

3. CARDOZO, RICHARD N. "Customer Satisfaction: Laboratory Study and Marketing Action," *Proceedings, Educators, Conference*, American Marketing Association, 1964.

4. FESTINGER, LEON. *A Theory of Cognitive Dissonance* (Stanford, Calif.: Stanford University Press), 1957.

5. HELSON, HARRY. "Current Trends and Issues in Adaptation-Level Theory," *American Psychologist*, Vol. 19 (January, 1964), pp. 26–38.

6. SPECTOR, AARON J. "Expectations, Fulfillment, and Morale," *Journal of Abnormal and Social Psychology*, Vol. 52 (January, 1956), pp. 51–56.

Name	Instructor
Date	Section

Problem 6-1

Refer to the experiments on "Shelf space and product sales in supermarkets" by Cox (see p. 33). In one of his experiments, he obtained the following results:*

Primary data collected from 6 by 6 latin-square test for Tang

	WEEKS										
	First		Second		Third		Fourth		Fifth		Sixth	
Stores	No. of shelves	Units sold	No. of shelves	Units sold	No. of shelves	Units sold	No. of shelves	Units sold	No. of shelves	Units sold	No. of shelves	Units sold
1	12	25	18	38	21	31	6	30	9	35	15	25
2	9	59	21	48	6	47	18	65	15	62	12	43
3	18	36	12	48	9	55	15	54	21	54	6	47
4	21	39	9	19	15	27	12	41	6	29	18	33
5	15	23	6	17	18	24	21	26	12	25	9	11
6	6	22	15	18	12	19	9	9	18	25	21	22

Note: In the test proceedings, the following code was used for the number of shelf spaces: A = 6, B = 9, C = 12, D = 15, E = 18, F = 21.

Analyze this data. From your analysis, what conclusions would you derive regarding shelf-space changes and product sales in supermarkets? Show your analysis in one or more tables.

*Keith K. Cox, *The Relationship Between Shelf Space and Product Sales in Supermarkets* (Austin: Bureau of Business Research, The University of Texas), 1964, p. 59.

Name   Instructor

Date   Section

Problem 6–2

Refer to the laboratory experiment "Effects of alternatives on buying decisions" on p. 76. The following table presents the results of this experiment. Analyze these results and present your interpretation and conclusions.*

Experimental conditions	N	Pre-mean rating	Post-mean rating
A. Two alternative conflict			
Chosen	13	6.50	6.66
Rejected	13	6.23	4.35
Difference			
B. Two alternative preference			
Chosen	19	6.74	6.66
Rejected	19	2.28	2.14
Difference			
C. Four alternative conflict			
Chosen	17	6.81	7.18
Rejected	17	6.79	4.95
Difference			
D. Four alternative preference			
Chosen	10	6.45	6.50
Rejected	10	3.00	1.85
Difference			

*Adapted from Lee K. Anderson, James R. Taylor, and Robert J. Holloway, "The Consumer and His Alternatives: An Experimental Approach," *Journal of Marketing Research*, Vol. III (February, 1966), pp. 66–67.

Name	Instructor
Date	Section

Problem 6-3

Identification of products and sponsors*

PERCENTAGE OF Ss MAKING CORRECT IDENTIFICATIONS

Group	Products		Sponsors	
	Ford Mustang	Retail groceries	Ford dealer	Supermarket
A	100	—	68	—
B	—	85	—	59
ab	85	84	25	44
ba	98	98	32	50

Group A: Shown 60-second Ford Mustang commercial for a Ford dealer
Group B: Shown 60-second food products commercial for a supermarket
Group ab: Shown 30-second version of Ford Mustang commercial, followed by 30-second version of the food commercial
Group ba: Shown 30-second food commercial followed by 30-second Ford Mustang commercial

*Adapted from John A. Martilla and Donald L. Thompson, "The Perceived Effects of 'Piggyback' Television Commercials," *Journal of Marketing Research*, Vol. III (November, 1966), p. 368.

Based on the above results, answer the following questions:

1. What was the problem being investigated?

2. What are the experimental treatments to which these results would seem to relate?

3. Analyze the results and indicate your conclusions.

7

Applications and implications

One of the goals of the experimenter in marketing is to apply his research findings to "real world" marketing. Improving the efficiency of marketing through research is beneficial to both businesses and consumers.

The applications and implications of research findings are not always obvious. The implications of the results as they apply to the hypotheses are, or should be, obvious; but there are frequently other implications to be drawn from the results.

Several years ago one of the authors published the results of a replication of the classical Asch conformity experiment.

It was decided that the first experiment should be a straightforward replication of a classical psychology experiment. The Asch study of conformity to group pressure was chosen. In this study, three students were told ahead of time to express concurrence as to which of three lines was the same length as another comparison line on 18 sets of judgments. They understood that they were to make deliberately incorrect decisions on 12 of the 18 trials. On each judgment, the three students expressed their estimates in the presence of a fourth, experimental, subject. Would the fourth subject give an incorrect response because three of his classmates made unanimous decisions incorrectly? As Asch had learned earlier, the experiment found that group pressures do cause subjects to give incorrect decisions even though they know their responses are contrary to fact, apparently because they do not want to appear "different." The CESB* [our] results are shown in

the figure in comparison to the original Asch results. It is apparent that the CESB results rather closely followed those of Asch. Some differences would be anticipated since the groups differed in several ways. Asch, for example, used only males whereas CESB used mixed groups.

Subsequent variations of this classic study tested the effects of stimuli to other sense modalities and all results were essentially the same. Whether judging the sweetness of cookies, the fragrance of perfumes, the tones of an organ, or the ripeness of fruit, a subject's objective appraisal was often subordinated to his apparent need to conform to others in the group.[1]

An advertising executive in Kansas City "tested" new consumer products by gathering a group of housewives around a table and having them pass a new item from person to person. Each housewife was to give a positive or negative comment on the item. Upon reading the above study, the executive realized that he could be setting up a conformity situation, so he "experimented." He set up two tables of housewives. At one table he secretly asked the first housewife who was going to comment to make a negative comment. At the other table he secretly asked the first housewife to comment to make a positive comment. Frequently he "replicated" the conformity experiment, and so he changed his technique of new product testing! The point is that this executive trained himself to watch for implications from research results that he could apply to his own marketing activities.

Sources of experimental studies

Experimental studies in marketing are most

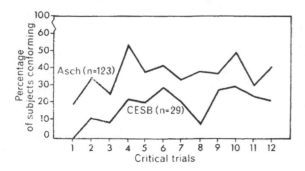

* CESB: Center for Experimental Studies in Business, University of Minnesota.

1. R. J. Holloway and T. White, "Advancing the Experimental Method in Marketing," *Journal of Marketing Research*, Vol. I (January, 1964), pp. 26–27.

frequently found in the following publications:

Journal of Marketing Research
Journal of Advertising Research
Journal of Marketing

Other business publications, such as the following, also carry experimental results from time to time:

Harvard Business Review
Journal of Business
Public Opinion Quarterly
Management Science
Applied Statistics
Journal of Applied Psychology

There is now a basic experimental bibliography available.[2] This publication has attempted to bring together, in one place, all the published experiments related to all areas of marketing. Students are urged to read as many experiments reported in this publication as possible to familiarize themselves with the type of experiments and experimental approaches used in investigating marketing problems.

This chapter provides the student with some practice in drawing marketing implications from results obtained by the experimental method. It is hoped that the student will "stretch" the research results as far as possible in order to find as many applications and implications as possible. To acquaint students further with some of the experimental work, several published articles are listed below under different marketing topics. Read the articles assigned by your instructor and answer the questions in the problem section for each topic:

I. CONSUMER BEHAVIOR

a. Perception

MAKENS, JAMES C. "Effect of Brand Preference Upon Consumers' Perceived Taste of Turkey Meat," *Journal of Applied Psychology*, Vol. 49, No. 4 (August, 1964), pp. 261–263.

NAYLOR, JAMES C. "Deceptive Packaging: Are the Deceivers Being Deceived?" *Journal of Applied Psychology*, Vol. 46, No. 6 (December, 1962), pp. 393–398.

BROWN, ROBERT L. "Wrapper Influence on the Perception of Freshness in Bread," *Journal of Applied Psychology*, Vol. 42 (1958), pp. 257–260.

b. Taste

ALLISON, RALPH I., and UHL, KENNETH P. "Influence of Beer Brand Identification on Taste Perception," *Journal of Marketing Research*, Vol. 1, No. 3 (August, 1964), pp. 36–39.

RAMOND, C. K., RACHAL, L. H. and MARKS, M. R. "Brand Discrimination Among Cigarette Smokers," *Journal of Applied Psychology*, Vol. 34, No. 5 (October, 1950), pp. 282–284.

THUMIN, FREDERICK J. "Identification of Cola Beverages, "*Journal of Applied Psychology*, Vol. 46, No. 5 (October, 1962), pp. 358–360.

c. Attitude

AUSTER, DONALD. "Attitude Change and Cognitive Dissonance," *Journal of Marketing Research*, Vol. 2, No. 4 (November, 1965), pp. 401–405.

ENGEL, JAMES F. "Are Automobile Purchasers Dissonant Consumers?" *Journal of Marketing*, Vol. 27, No. 2 (April, 1963), pp. 55–58.

GREENE, JEROME, and STOCK, STEVENS. "Brand Attitudes as Measures of Advertising Effect," *Journal of Advertising Research*, Vol. 6, No. 2 (June, 1966), pp. 14–22.

d. Personal influence

STAFFORD, JAMES E. "Effects of Group Influences on Consumer Brand Preferences," *Journal of Marketing Research*, Vol. 3, No. 1 (February, 1966), pp. 68–75.

VENKATESAN, M. "An Experimental Investigation in the Conditions Producing Conformity to and Independence of Group Norms in Consumer Behavior," *Journal of Marketing Research*, Vol. 3, No. 4 (November, 1966), pp. 384–387.

GRUEN, WALTER. "Preference for New Products and Its Relationship to Different Measures of Conformity," *Journal of Applied Psychology*, Vol. 44, No. 6 (December, 1960), pp. 361–364.

II. PRODUCT RESEARCH

PAYNE, DONALD E. "Jet Set, Pseudo-Store, and New Product Testing," *Journal of Marketing Research*, Vol. 3, No. 4 (November, 1966), pp. 372–376.

BENGSTON, ROGER, and BRENNER, HENRY. "Product Test Results Using Three different Methodologies," *Journal of Marketing Research*, Vol. I, No. 4 (November, 1964), pp. 49–52.

III. PRICING

LEAVITT, HAROLD J. "A Note on Some Experimental Findings About the Meanings of Price," *Journal of Business*, Vol. 27, No. 3 (July, 1954), pp. 205–210.

TULL, D. S., BORING, R. A., and CONSIOR, M. H. "A Note on the Relationship of Price and Imputed Quality," *Journal of Business*, Vol. 37, No. 2 (April, 1964), pp. 186–191.

McCONNELL, J. DOUGLAS. "The Price-Quality Relationship in an Experimental Setting," *Journal of Marketing Research*, Vol. V (August, 1968), pp. 300–303.

---

2. Robert J. Holloway, ed., *Experiments in Marketing*, Bibliography Series No. 14 (Chicago, Ill.: American Marketing Association), 1967.

IV. PERSUASION

a. *Advertising*

BECKNELL, JAMES C., Jr., and McISAAC, ROBERT W. "Test Marketing Cookware Coated with 'Teflon,'" *Journal of Advertising Research*, Vol. 3, No. 3 (September, 1963), pp. 2–8.

GARDNER, DAVID M., "The effect of Divided Attention on Attitude Changes Induced by Persuasive Marketing Communications," in *Science, Technology, and Marketing*, ed. by Richard M. Haas. Chicago: American Marketing Association, 1966, pp. 532–540.

BARBAN, ARNOLD M., and CUNDIFF, EDWARD W., "Negro and White Response to Advertising Stimuli," *Journal of Marketing Research*, Vol. I, No. 4 (November, 1964), pp. 53–56.

ROBINSON, EDWARD J. "How an Advertisement's Size Affects Responses to It," *Journal of Advertising Research*, Vol. 3, No. 4 (December, 1963), pp. 16–25.

b. *Personal selling*

LEVITT, T. "Communications and Industrial Selling," *Journal of Marketing*, Vol. 31 (April, 1967), pp. 15–21.

HUGHES, G. DAVID. "A New Tool for Sales Managers," *Journal of Marketing Research*, Vol. 1, No. 2 (May, 1964), pp. 32–38.

PACE, R. WAYNE. "Oral Communication and Sales Effectiveness," *Journal of Applied Psychology*, Vol. 46, No. 5 (1962), pp. 321–324.

c. *Merchandising*

COX, K., "The Responsiveness of Food Sales to Supermarket Shelf Space Changes," *Journal of Marketing Research*, Vol. I (May, 1964), pp. 63–67.

FARRELL, K. "Effects of Point-of-Sale Promotional Material on Sales of Cantaloupes," *Journal of Advertising Research*, Vol. 5 (December, 1965), pp. 8–12.

V. MARKETING RESEARCH

KIMBALL, ANDREW E. "Increasing the Rate of Return in Mail Surveys," *Journal of Marketing*, Vol. 25, No. 6 (October, 1961), pp. 63–64.

BENGSTON, ROGER, and BRENNER, HENRY. "Product Test Results Using Three Different Methodologies," *Journal of Marketing Research*, Vol. 1. No. 4 (November, 1964), pp. 49–52.

FORD, NEIL M. "The Advance Letter in Mail Surveys," *Journal of Marketing Research*, Vol. 4, No, 2 (May, 1967), pp. 202–204.

Name   Instructor

Date   Section

Problem 7–1 Perception

Article assigned: _____

1. Restate the problem(s) in simple marketing terms:

2. Explain the results in marketing terms and in your own words:

3. List all the marketing implications that can be drawn from the study:

Problem 7–2 Taste

Article assigned: _____

1. Restate the problem(s) in simple marketing terms:

2. Explain the results in marketing terms and in your own words:

3. List all the marketing implications that can be drawn from the study:

Name	Instructor
Date	Section

Problem 7-3 Attitude

Article assigned: _____

1. Restate the problem(s) in simple marketing terms:

2. Explain the results in marketing terms and in your own words:

3. List all the marketing implications that can be drawn from the study:

Problem 7–4 Personal influence

Article assigned: _____

1. Restate the problem(s) in simple marketing terms:

2. Explain the results in marketing terms and in your own words:

3. List all the marketing implications that can be drawn from the study:

Name   Instructor

Date   Section

Problem 7–5 Product research

Article assigned:

1. Restate the problem(s) in simple marketing terms:

2. Explain the results in marketing terms and in your own words:

3. List all the marketing implications that can be drawn from the study:

Problem 7–6 Pricing

Article assigned: _____

1. Restate the problem(s) in simple marketing terms:

2. Explain the results in marketing terms and in your own words:

3. List all the marketing implications that can be drawn from the study:

Name   Instructor

Date   Section

Problem 7–7 Advertising

Article assigned: _____

1. Restate the problem(s) in simple marketing terms:

2. Explain the results in marketing terms and in your own words:

3. List all the marketing implications that can be drawn from the study:

Problem 7–8 Personal selling

Article assigned: _____

1. Restate the problem(s) in simple marketing terms:

2. Explain the results in marketing terms and in your own words:

3. List all the marketing implications that can be drawn from the study:

Name   Instructor

Date   Section

Problem 7–9 Merchandising

Article assigned: _____

1. Restate the problem(s) in simple marketing terms:

2. Explain the results in marketing terms and in your own words:

3. List all the marketing implications that can be drawn from the study:

Problem 7–10 Marketing research

Article assigned: _____

1. Restate the problem(s) in simple marketing terms:

2. Explain the results in marketing terms and in your own words:

3. List all the marketing implications that can be drawn from the study:

APPENDIX A

Appendix A: Mechanical measures

In Chapter 3 we demonstrated how useful special apparatus and methods can be in marketing experimentation. The figures and descriptions in this Appendix should further illustrate their value.

Eye pupil measurement

Both the apparatus and the method involved were introduced in Chapter 3. To be more specific: These are utilized to record pupillary responses to sensory, mental, and emotional stimulation.

Figure A–1 illustrates the procedure of measurement. The subject looks through the aperture and the pupil-response apparatus camera films her pupillary response. The switches on the box control the apparatus's internal illumination, the camera, and the slide projector.

Figure A–2 is a five-frame series of pictures showing the eye of a male subject during the first 2.5 seconds after a photo of a pinup girl appeared on the screen of the pupil apparatus.

Recording eye movements

The eye-movement camera (not shown) was

1. Donald Payne, "Looking without learning: Eye movements when viewing print advertisements," in *Marketing for Tomorrow Today*, M. S. Moyer and R. S. Vosburgh (editors). Proceedings of the June, 1967 Conference of the American Marketing Association (Series No. 25), Chicago, Ill., 1967, pp. 78ff.
2. Edward J. Robinson, "How an Advertisement's Size Affects Responses to It," *Journal of Advertising Research*, Vol. 3 (December 1963), p. 19. © Advertising Research Foundation, Inc., 1963.
3. Edwin Golin and Samuel B. Lyerly, "The Galvanic Skin Response as a Test of Advertising Impact," *Journal of Applied Psychology*, Vol. 34 (December, 1950), p. 440. Copyright 1950 by the American Psychological Association, and reproduced by permission.

originally developed by Norman Mackworth. This device simultaneously photographs both the scene which is exposed to the subject's view, and the specific point within that scene at which the subject is looking. A record is made, by reflecting a spot of light off the cornea of the eye, which shows where the subject was looking.[1]

Figure A–3 is an example of recorded eye-movement patterns.[2]

Measuring galvanic skin response (GSR)

...the GSR results from changes in skin resistance to an induced current. These changes of resistance may be read off a scale by deflections from a mirror galvanometer. It is assumed by many investigators that the GSR is a reflection of general autonomic nervous activity and that autonomic activity accompanies emotional states; hence GSR may be considered as one possible index of emotion. Applied to an advertisement, then, a layout of highly affective components for any particular observer should result in greater GSR deflections than a less affective one.[3]

Operant conditioning device

The *consumer's enclosure* is schematically diagrammed, along with the other very important apparatus components, in Figure A–4. The enclosure can be any comfortably air-conditioned room which isolates the experimental consumer from other individuals and unwanted variables which might disturb his viewing behavior. Our experimental rooms are painted blue and are equipped with comfortable chairs for the viewer. Mounted in the wall approximately six feet from the viewer is the television receiver, whose brightness the consumer controls. The consumer can hold in either hand a small switch which produces a brief (less than 0.5 second), slight increase in the brightness of the television image. Even if the switch is held down, only this brief period of

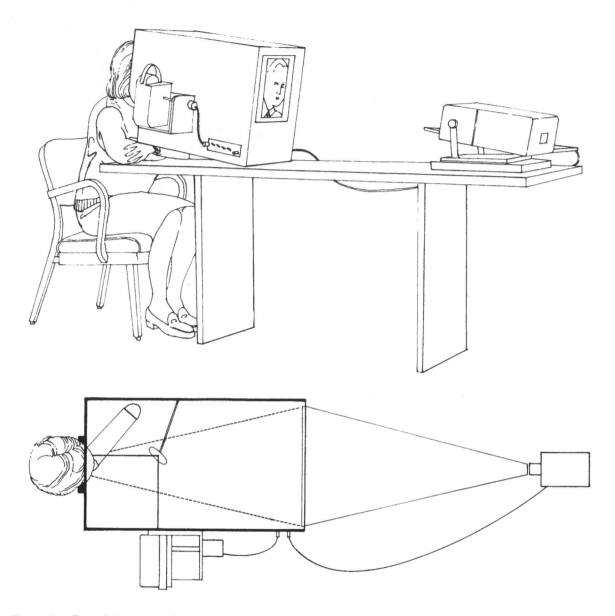

Figure A–1. Top: *Subject in pupil-response studies views slides flashed onto screen by projector. Motor-driven camera attached to apparatus records pupil size at rate of two frames per second.*

Bottom: *The pupil-response apparatus's lamp and camera utilize infrared light; the mirror is below eye level to afford an unobstructed view of the screen. The projector changes pictures every ten seconds, alternately flashing a control slide and then a stimulus slide.*

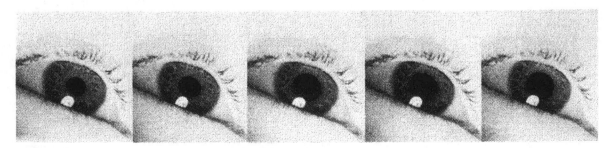

Figure A–2. *A picture of a pinup girl caused a male subject's pupil diameter to increase 30 per cent in 2.5 seconds.* Photos courtesy of Eckhard H. Hess.

illumination is permitted. The *response definer* converts each press of the switch to an electrical pulse which operates the *conjugate reinforcer*. Thus high rates of responding (above 60 per minute) keep the picture brightly illuminated for comfortable viewing; intermediate rates of responding keep the picture at dimmer levels; and during periods of no responding the picture tube is dark.

The audio part of the television program is continuously presented to the consumer through comfortable earphones. Earphones are used so that his vocal responses (e.g., laughing) can be recorded by a microphone within the room without also picking up the responses of the television audience.

The *experimenter's monitors* consist of earphones, one (labeled "P" in Figure A-4) through which the experimenter can hear the audio part of the television program and another (labeled "C") through which he can hear the vocal responses of the consumer. The experimenter also has a television receiver equipped with a monitoring switch so that he may view either the program the consumer has an opportunity to see or the image on the consumer's receiver produced by his responses. The use of these monitors permits the experimenter to check when the consumer is not responding to see if it is because the set is out of tune or because the consumer is not interested in looking at a clear image.

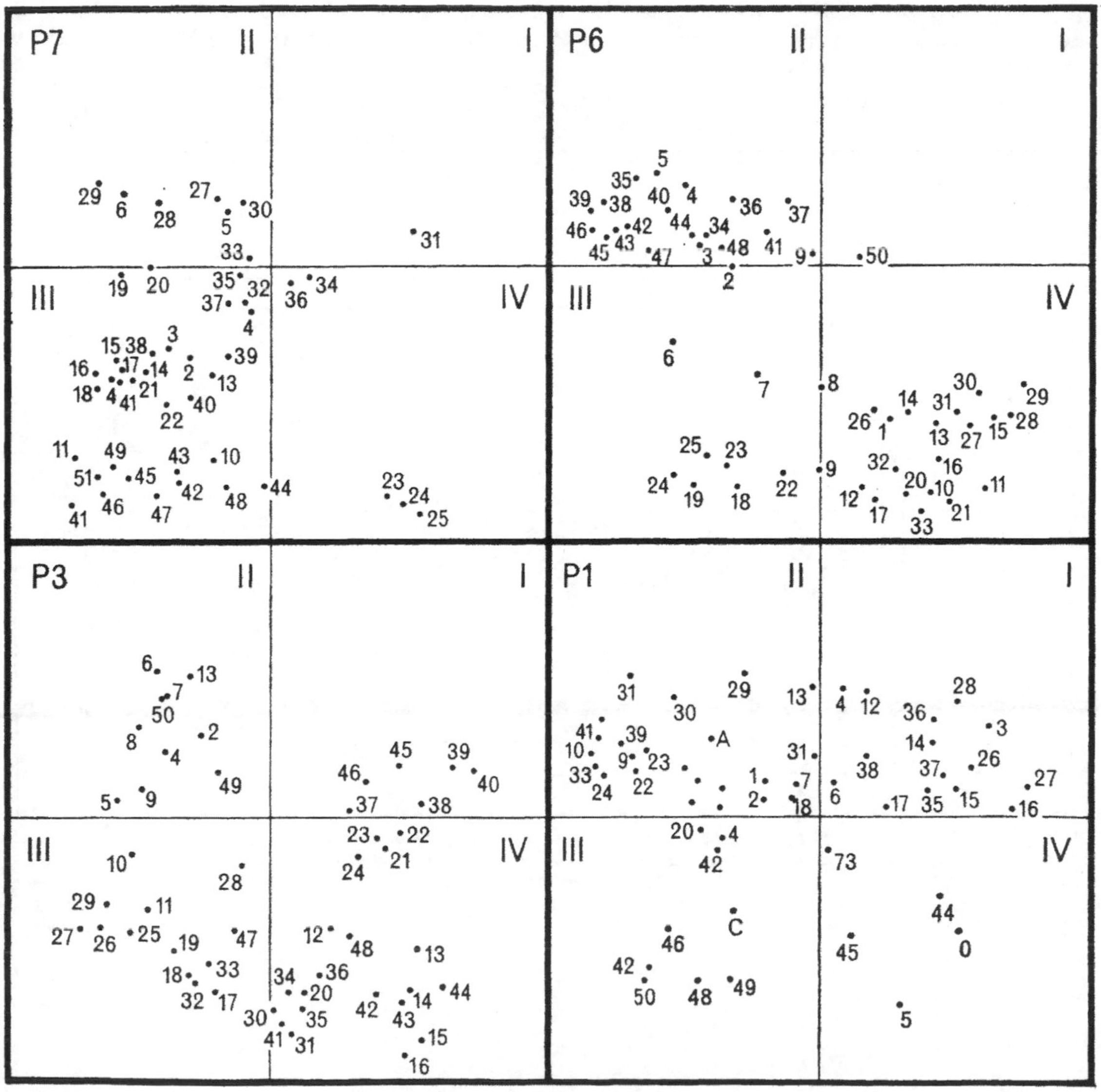

Figure A-3. *Eye-movement patterns for one subject viewing four large ads.* After Robinson (Fig. 3) in *Journal of Advertising Research.*

Consumer's operant response rate is recorded on the *cumulative response recorder* (diagrammed in Figure A–4 and described above). The slope of the line on these records indicates the rate of pressing the switch and the brightness of the consumer's receiver. These records provide a direct measure of the consumer's moment-to-moment interest, or desire to work for the video portion of the television program. In other words, they are records of his looking responses. The experimenter can indicate anything of interest on these records by pressing a switch which moves the pen to the right and downward, making a "hatch" mark on the record. In the figures in this article these hatch marks indicate the beginning and end of commercials appearing in a television program. If the experimenter wishes, he can also write on the cumulative response record any changes in program content, etc.

Consumer's vocal responses are recorded through the microphone in the consumer's enclosure onto one channel of a *stereophonic tape*

recorder. At the end of the program additional responses are obtained from the consumer by having him fill out a questionnaire and by interviewing him. However, these questionnaire and interview results suffer from recall bias, even though the recall is almost immediate. Our data have shown that the results of these interviews are by no means as accurate, subtle, or sensitive to moment-to-moment changes in viewing behavior as is the directly recorded operant response.

Copy content is recorded on the second channel of the stereophonic tape recorder. It is also possible to record the video content on a video tape recorder. These records of copy content can then be compared with the cumulative response record and the consumer's vocal response record for moment-to-moment analysis.[4]

4. Ogden R. Lindsley, "A Behavioral Measure of Television Viewing," *Journal of Advertising Research*, Vol. 2 (September, 1962), pp. 4–5. © Advertising Research Foundation, Inc., 1962.

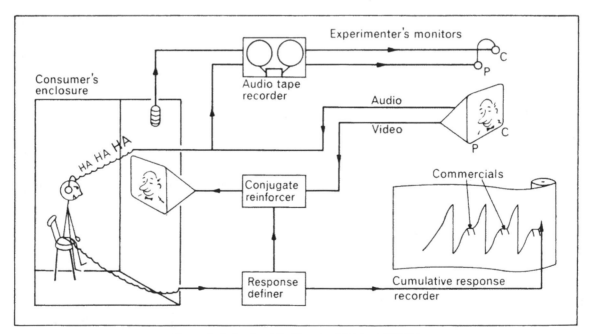

Figure A–4. *A schematic diagram of the experimental room.* Adapted from Lindsley (Fig. 1) in *Journal of Advertising Research.*

Appendix B:
Validity of experiments

Internal and external validity of experiments[1]

Campbell, in discussing research design, concentrates on two areas: *internal validity* and *external validity*.

Internal validity is concerned with the issue of whether or not the specific treatment in which the researcher is interested has actually brought about the effect indicated by the measuring devices.

In discussions of factors affecting the internal validity of experiments, we shall attempt to discover whether there are logical, plausible alternate explanations for the effect measured by the researcher other than the treatments he applied to this test units. Only if it is clear that no other hypothesis is tenable shall we be willing to accept the experimental treatments as *the* causal factor in the experimental situation. This is a process analogous to the statistical testing of null hypotheses.

External validity deals with the problem of projecting one's results from the experimental setting to the world: To what populations, settings, and treatment and measurement variables can be projected a given finding from the research design?

Both types of criteria are obviously important: They both must be evaluated if our research is to be acted upon. Actually, the effects of internal and external validity variables may work at cross-purposes. Lab experimentation usually means greater control over factors affecting internal validity, but it raises the whole issue of the ability of the experimenter to extrapolate from his precise laboratory situation to competitive conditions of the real world. Experimental design which maximizes control over factors affecting external validity may not provide sufficient internal validity, or may result in experiments under which it is hard to measure internal validity. Obviously, the researcher's goal should be the creation of a design for each particular problem which will be strong in both types of validity.

Factors jeopardizing internal and external validity[2]

Fundamental to this listing is a distinction between internal validity and external validity. Internal validity is the basic minimum without which any experiment is uninterpretable: Did in fact the experimental treatments make a difference in this specific experimental instance? External validity asks the question of generalizability: To what populations, settings, treatment variables, and measurement variables can this effect be generalized? Both types of criteria are obviously important, even though they are frequently at odds in that features increasing one may jeopardize the other. While internal validity is the *sine qua non,* and while the question of external validity, like the question of inductive inference, is never completely answerable, the selection of designs strong in both types of validity is obviously our ideal. This is particularly the case for research on teaching, in which generalization to applied settings of known character is the desideratum. Both the distinctions and the relations between these two classes of validity considerations will be made more explicit as they are illustrated in the discussions of specific designs.

Relevant to *internal validity*, eight different classes of extraneous variables will be presented; these variables, if not controlled in the experimental design, might produce effects confounded with the effect of the experimental stimulus. They represent the effects of:

1. *History,* the specific events occurring between the first and second measurement in addition to the experimental variable.

---

1. Seymour Banks, *Experimentation in Marketing.* Copyright 1965 (New York: McGraw-Hill Book Company), p. 26. Used with permission of McGraw-Hill Book Company.

2. Donald T. Campbell and J. C. Stanley, "Experimental and Quasi-experimental Designs for Research on Teaching," in N. L. Gage (editor), *Handbook of Research on Teaching* (Chicago, Ill.: Rand McNally), 1963, pp. 171–246.

2. *Maturation,* processes within the respondents operating as a function of the passage of time *per se* (not specific to the particular events), including growing older, growing hungrier, growing more tired, and the like.

3. *Testing,* the effects of taking a test upon the scores of a second testing.

4. *Instrumentation,* in which changes in the calibration of a measuring instrument or changes in the observers or scores used may produce changes in the obtained measurements.

5. *Statistical regression,* operating where groups have been selected on the basis of their extreme scores.

6. *Biases* resulting in differential selection of respondents for the comparison groups.

7. *Experimental mortality,* or differential loss of respondents from the comparison groups.

8. *Selection-maturation interaction,* etc., which in certain of the multiple-group quasi-experimental designs, such as Design 10, is confounded with, i.e., might be mistaken for, the effect of the experimental variable.

The factors jeopardizing external validity or representativeness which will be discussed are:

9. The reactive or interaction effect of *testing,* in which a pretest might increase or decrease the respondent's sensitivity or responsiveness to the experimental variable and thus make the results obtained for a pretested population unrepresentative of the effects of the experimental variable for the unpretested universe from which the experimental respondents were selected.

10. The interaction effects of *selection biases* and the experimental variable.

11. Reactive effects of *experimental arrangements,* which would preclude generalization about the effect of the experimental variable upon persons being exposed to it in nonexperimental settings.

12. *Multiple-treatment interference,* likely to occur whenever multiple treatments are applied to the same respondents, because the effects of prior treatments are not usually erasable.

Appendix C: Laboratory experiments in marketing: the experimenter effect[*]

M. VENKATESAN

Holloway and White (12) have emphasized the need for advancing the experimental method in marketing. Since then Holloway and his students have pioneered in the application of controlled laboratory methods for investigating fundamental marketing problems (1, 5, 8, 9, 10, 11, 17, 31, 32). Many marketing problems are being investigated using the laboratory method. It is evident from the increasing number of articles in *JMR* that experimental research in the field is also becoming one of the important techniques for marketing researchers.

Prediction has a significant role in scientific method. However, as Westley observed, "It is not the obtained verifications but the verifiability of its methodological procedures that establishes a discipline's pretensions for scientific status (33, p. 246)." This verifiability is maximized by the use of laboratory method, for this methodology is conducive to true replications. If the key characteristic difference between experimental and nonexperimental inquiry is largely the degree of control, then the laboratory situation presumably provides full control of variables not under investigation. Then the responses obtained result from the manipulation of the experimental variable(s). Any unintended or unexpected variation in the behavior of the

subjects is regarded as an error. As Rosenthall (24, p. 256) observed, "Whether we will ever be able to nail down all the sources of variance in a transactional data collection system is one of the philosophical questions." However, any attempt to understand the sources of unintended variation and ways of combating them will increase the usefulness of the experimental methodology.

This article is restricted to the mediation of experimenter effect or bias in controlled laboratory experimentation.[1] The problems encountered in experimental methods have received considerable attention. For example, the detection and correction of interviewer bias has been extensively researched, and there is much literature in this area (3, 4, 6, 13, 15). This article is confined to laboratory methodology to present recent research findings from experimental social psychology. Though the problems of experimenter bias were recognized as early as 1904 (14), only in the last 10 years has it been systematically studied. Researchers in marketing are learning

---

1. Attempts have been made recently to separate experimenter bias from experimenter effect. For example, when different experimenters obtain different data from comparable subjects, the phenomenon is known as "experimenter effect," whereas "experimenter bias" occurs when experimenters obtain the data that they expect to obtain. At present, there is no clear distinction between experimenter effect and experimenter bias. Therefore, in this article, the terms are synonymous.

*Reprinted with permission, from *Journal of Marketing Research*, Vol. IV (May, 1967), pp. 142–146.

laboratory methodology, and thus an awareness of the phenomenon of experimenter bias will help their designs and advance the methodology more effectively.

In behavioral research it has been accepted that the experimenter was necessary and harmless and that he had little influence on the subjects' responses. The subjects were viewed as passive responders to stimuli. The experimenter was not studied as an independent variable but as McGuigan (16) said he was "the neglected stimulus object."

Riecken (19) sees the process of collecting data about human behavior in an experimental situation as a special form of social interaction, with a typical experiment having the following features:

1. It is invitational: most participating subjects are volunteers.
2. The nature of the invitational terms are unspecified.
3. Status relationship exists between the experimenter (E) and the subject (S).
4. It is temporally and spatially set apart from daily life.
5. The distribution of information is one-sided.

In such a situation, said Reicken (19), the subject tries, at any particular point in the sequence of events of an experiment, to form a definition of the experimental situation.

One peculiar, striking characteristic of the experimental situation is the high degree of control over the subject in the E–S relationship. Orne (18) points out that the typical subject respects science and thus tolerates a considerable degree of discomfort, boredom, etc. He illustrates the extent of experimenter control by the following example: In one experiment, the subjects were to perform serial additions of each adjacent two numbers on sheets filled with rows of random digits; to complete one sheet, 224 additions were required. Each subject received a stack of 2,000 sheets and had instructions to continue work until the experimenter returned. The subjects were deprived of their watches. Five and one-half hours later, the experimenter gave up. The subjects tended to continue to perform this boring task. Similar examples by Orne

demonstrate the degree of control the experimenter has over his subjects.

Orne viewed the subject's performance in an experiment as problem-solving behavior, where the total cues become significant determinants of subject's behavior. The total of such cues is the "demand characteristics of the experimental situation." Orne (18) and Riecken (19) forcefully pointed out that the assumptions about the experimenter having no influence on the subjects' responses or the subjects as passive responders in the experimental situation are invalid and unjustified. Thus Orne proposed that a subject's behavior in any experimental situation is determined by two sets of variables: (a) experimental variables, and (b) perceived demand characteristics of the experimental situation. This and other proposals have labeled the subject an active participant in this social interaction, and thus his behavior must be viewed in the total setting of an experimental situation. In such a situation, the experimenter can not be regarded as a necessary but harmless element. His influence, his effect, and his bias must be studied systematically as partial determinants of research results.

According to Rosenthal and Fode (25), there are three sources for experimenters' influence on subjects: (a) designed-conscious source of influence; (b) undesigned-conscious source of influence, and (c) undesigned-unconscious source of influence. Rosenthal (20) separates public biases of the experimenter that are known from private biases that are unknown. The experimenter's public biases are his selection of a particular area for research, selection of a particular design, etc. "Events occuring in the S–E relationship are at best only partly public—E can tell us only what he knows he did to S. He cannot tell us of any effect he may have had on S of which he is unaware (20, p. 662)." This undesigned-unconscious source of influence of the experimenter is the "unconscious experimenter" bias.

Present research indicates the following main sources of experimenter bias: experimenter expectancy and his outcome-orientation, the effects of early data returns, desirability of data, modeling effects of the experimenter; personality, sex, and other attributes of the experimenter. Little is known about many of these effects, and only recently systematic studies of experimenter effects have begun. Major findings are reviewed, and implications for experimental studies in marketing are considered.

Research findings

EXPERIMENTER EXPECTATION

A series of experiments recently reported suggest that experimenter's expectancy or hypothesis may be a significant partial determinant of the results he obtains. In a person-perception experiment (7), subjects were required to rate the degree of success or failure of people pictured in photographs. The experimenters in this study were lead to expect ratings of success from some subjects and ratings of failure from some. Unknown to the experimenters, the subjects were randomly assigned to the success-perceiving and failure-perceiving groups. The results indicated that the experimenters obtained ratings from their subjects according to the (E's) expectancy, regardless of the particular kind of expectancy.

In another experiment (25) involving the same person-perception task, half the experimenters were told to expect a high rating (an average of 5 rating on 10 neutral photographs) from their subjects, and the matched other half of the experimenters were told to expect a low rating (average −5 rating) from their subjects. The extent of difference among ratings obtained by the experimenters in the two conditions follows:

Experimenter group	High bias (+5)		Low bias (−5)	
	N	Mean rating	N	Mean rating
A	19	3.47	21	1.81
B	20	6.60	24	−3.71
C	21	4.48	22	−4.23
D	18	2.50	20	1.70
E	21	3.05	20	0.40

Thus, the experimenters obtained higher or lower mean ratings relating to their experimentally induced expectation.

The effect of expectancy was demonstrated in a study using teachers (28).

Teachers were told that 20 percent of the children in 18 classrooms had unusual potential for intellectual gains, shown by a previously conducted test. That percentage of children had in fact been selected at random. Eight months later these children showed significantly greater gains in I.Q. than did other children in the control group. These gains are seen in the percentages of children in the control and experimental groups who gained I.Q. points. For example, among first and second grade children, 49 percent in the control versus 79 percent in the experimental group gained at least 10 points, 19 percent in the control and 47 percent in the experimental group gained at least 20 points, while the percentages are 5 and 21 of the groups gaining 30 or more points.

Other experiments (21, 29) confirm this evidence that the experimenter's expectation determines, to a significant extent, the extent of the data he obtains.

In most experimental situations, the experimenter has some orientation about the outcome or results. This orientation (experimenter's expectations and wishes) can affect the data from experimental research as Rosenthal reported (23).

EARLY DATA RETURNS

In any experimental situation, the experimenter receives information through early data returns that may contaminate the subsequent data. To test this hypothesis of the effect of early data returns on subsequent data, Rosenthal, *et al.* (26), biased 12 experimenters, each studying six subjects on a photo-rating task. The experimenters were randomly divided into three treatment groups. By using two accomplices, the first two subjects handled by the experimenter, one group of experimenters was made to obtain good or expected data. Likewise, the second group of experimenters was made to obtain bad or unexpected data from their first two subjects. The other four subjects of experimenters in these two groups were naive subjects. For the third group of experimenters, the control group, all six assigned subjects were naive.

Results indicated that the experimenters obtaining good initial data also had better subsequent data. Similarly, the experimenters, who obtained bad initial data, tended to obtain worse subsequent data. For example, the mean ratings from the four subjects assigned to each of the four experimenters in the good data group was .80; the mean rating for the bad data group was .18; for the control group it was .58.

The effects of the early data in obtaining subsequent data become clear when the mean ratings for the first two subjects versus the last two subjects are examined. In the good data group, the mean rating by the first two subjects was .58 as compared with 1.02 for the last two subjects; comparable data for the bad data group was .47 and −.12. The study concluded that the flow of early data affected the experimenter's expectation of the data he subsequently obtains.

EXPERIMENTER MODELING

Rosenthal defined modeling as: "The extent to which a given experimenter's own performance of an experimental task determines his subjects' performance of the same task is the extent to which the experimenter 'models' his subjects (22, p. 467)." Eight experiments were conducted, using the same task, that required rating a series of photographs on a scale of how successful or unsuccessful the pictured person seemed. Before using the subjects, the experimenters were to rate the same pictures. Modeling effects were measured by the correlation between the mean rating of the photos by the experimenters and the mean photo ratings then obtained by them from their subjects.

The rank-order correlations between the experimenters' ratings and their subjects' ratings ranged from −.49 to +.65. Although it is difficult to demonstrate modeling effects in one experiment, Rosenthal and his associates pointed out that modeling effects may systematically affect the results of experiments. Thus Rosenthal observed that "it seems more likely than not that in different experiments utilizing a person-per-ception task, there will be significantly different magnitudes of modeling effects which for any single experiment might often be regarded as a chance fluctuation from a correlation of zero (21, p. 274)."

EXPERIMENTER ATTRIBUTES

There is some evidence that a variety of experimenter's attributes may act as partial determinants of subjects' responses. Although some studies have found that, in studies involving children, female experimenters could better control responses than male experimenters, in most studies conducted by Rosenthal and his associates no sex effect was revealed (21).

Experimenter's warmth, likability and other personality characteristics affect subjects' responses. In one study (7), experimenters whose behavior reflected greater competence, greater personal involvement, and a professional manner had ratings more related to their expectancy. Need for approval, anxiety level and other personality measures were related to experimenter bias in some situations (21).

Experimenter's status or perceived status was related to experimenter bias. Birney (2) found that a faculty experimenter induces different performance levels in subjects from those a graduate student experimenter does.

Mediation of experimenter effect

As indicated, the experimenter is unaware of these biases which are not caused by deliberate dishonesty. Then how is bias mediated? Both visual and verbal cues are pertinent.

In an experiment specially designed to study the transmission of cues (25), experimenters were divided randomly into two groups: one group for non-visual bias and the other for non-verbal bias. Subjects had a person-perception task. In the non-visual condition, the experimenter sat behind a screen across a table from the subjects, read the instructions, and recorded the subjects' ratings. In the non-verbal condition, the experimenter handed his subjects a sheet of instructions and remained silent until the task was completed.

The results indicated that both visual and verbal cues transmit bias. Elimination of visual cues reduced but did not eliminate the bias. In another study (7), sound motion pictures were made of experimenters conducting an experiment. The results from these studies suggest that visual cues are important but probably to a lesser extent than verbal cues.

In one study (30), the instruction-reading behavior of male experimenters greatly affected the data. The tone of voice, inflection, gestures, posture, and tempo not only contributed to the variation in experimenter behavior, but also resulted in unintentional communication of expectancies.

The subtle transmission of experimenter bias is clearly shown in this experiment (27): half the experimenters were biased to expect high ratings from their subjects, and the other half expected low ratings. At the conclusion of this phase, each experimenter was to train two research assistants and to keep them ignorant of any hypothesis. A subtle transmission was found of experimenter's bias to the research assistants, who influenced the responses of the subjects. Thus, a research assistant acting as an experimenter may be a carrier for the non-present influencer.

Implications for marketing experiments

The methodological implications for behavioral research suggested by Rosenthal (21) have much relevance to laboratory experiments in marketing. Hypotheses for many consumer behavior experimenters are derived from social psychological findings. For example, in evaluating the effect of the number of choices offered to the consumer, hypotheses are derived from the theory of cognitive dissonance. Other studies have formulated hypotheses based on dissonance theory, contrast theory and generally from research findings of social psychology. In these experiments, outcome orientation may have been a built-in factor. Moreover, marketing researchers favor differing theories from psychology to explain consumer behavior, and thus the confirma-

tion of their hypotheses may be heavily influenced by experimenter bias.

As shown, even when the research assistant was kept ignorant of the hypothesis, experimenter bias was subtly transmitted to the subjects. Hence, the practice of discussing the entire research project, including hypotheses and expectations, with research assistants may need changing if research assistants are to conduct experiments. The graduate student who runs his own experiment for thesis preparation is not only aware of his hypothesis but hopes desperately to prove his point to acquire his master's or doctorate degree.

In most marketing experiments mentioned (1, 5, 9, 17, 31, 32), the experimenter formulated the hypothesis. In some studies, research assistants conducting the experiments were on a team that formulated the hypotheses (10, 11); the operation of experimenter bias in such situations is beyond question.

In the expanding literature on laboratory controlled marketing experiments, no one mentions whether a single experimenter or a group conducted the study nor mentions whether the researcher, aware of his hypotheses, conducted the experiments. No longer is it sufficient to state, in the methodological section of the article, that instructions were given to the subjects, but the questions—whether the instructions were read by one or more experimenters, whether the instructions were standardized, and whether any improvisations by the experimenter were allowed—should be satisfactorily answered.

Graduate students or faculty members as marketing experimenters may not be aware of the subtle influences transmitted by instruction reading behavior, physical characteristics, etc. For example, if in an experimental situation one group of subjects is contacted by an experimenter wearing a suit while a second group of subjects is contacted later by an experimenter working in his shirt sleeves, the data may be affected by the experimenter's appearances. These subtle mechanics of experimentation need attention.

How can experimenter bias be reduced?

Standardized instructions and minimum improvisations by the experimenter may help. Counterbalancing experimenters may also help. The important control should be on the experimenters. The person who participates in formulating the hypothesis or who is aware of it should not train other research experimenters, nor should he contact subjects. As far as feasible, visual and verbal cues should be eliminated. Occasional monitoring of marketing experiments by observers to detect peculiarities in the situation or deviations from procedure would greatly add to control of experimenter bias. Since marketing researchers may have certain attitudes, predispositions, or expectations, attempts should be made to measure the experimenter's attitudes before he interacts with the subjects.

As suggested for interviewers, in the laboratory situation experimenters with known biases may be used. The blind techniques in the psychopharmacology research may also be applicable. In drug research, for example, a placebo experimental condition is created, and thus the physician is blind about a drug's being placebo or active. The blind and double-blind techniques in medical research can also be effectively used in marketing experiments.

Statistical techniques, such as partial correlation and covariance analysis, are available to assess the effects of experimenter bias in the collected data and to aid in data correction. Marketing experiments can use factorial designs in which the experimenter is treated as a variable. Automated data collection systems, when possible, such as taperecorded instructions, automatic record of responses, etc., can also be used.

Friedman, Kurland, and Rosenthal (7) suggest a special form of control, viz., the expectancy control group. In this procedure the experimental and control groups are subdivided, and half the subjects in the experimental condition are contacted by an experimenter who expects no critical response; contrarily, half the control group subjects are contacted by an experimenter who expects critical response. Analysis of these results can aid in the assessment of experimenter effects and correction of bias.

It is important that the marketing researcher assume the attitudes and practices of the clinicians to become aware of experimenter bias in laboratory experimentation and try to reduce this bias. Only by improved methodology can marketing researchers hope to advance experimental method and thus the science of marketing.

REFERENCES

1. ANDERSON, L. K., TAYLOR, J. R., and HOLLOWAY R. J. "The Consumer and His Alternatives: An Experimental Approach," *Journal of Marketing Research*, Vol. 3 (February, 1966), pp. 62–67.
2. BIRNEY, R. C. "The Achievement Motive and Task Performance: A Replication," *Journal of Abnormal Social Psychology*, Vol. 56 (January, 1958), pp. 133–135.
3. BLANKENSHIP, A. B. "The Effect of the Interviewer Upon the Response in a Public Opinion Poll," *Journal of Consulting Psychologist*, Vol. 4 (July–August, 1940), pp. 134–136.
4. BOYD, HARPER W., Jr., and WESTFALL, RALPH. "Interviewers as a Source of Error," *Journal of Marketings*. Vol. 19 (April, 1955), pp. 311–324.
5. CARDOZO, RICHARD N. "An Experimental Study of Customer Effort, Expectation, and Satisfaction," *Journal of Marketing Research*, Vol. 2 (August, 1965), pp. 244–249.
6. FERBER, ROBERT, and WALES, HUGH G. "Detection and Correction of Interviewer Bias," *Public Opinion Quarterly*, Vol. 16 (Spring, 1952), pp. 107–127.
7. FRIEDMAN, NEIL, KURLAND, DANIEL, and ROSENTHAL, ROBERT. "Experimenter Behavior as an Unintended Determinant of Experimental Results," *Journal of Projective Techniques and Personality Assessment*, Vol. 29 (December, 1965), pp. 479–490.
8. GARDNER, DAVID M. "The Effect of Divided Attention on Attitude Change Induced by a Persuasive Marketing Communication," Paper presented at Fall Meeting, American Marketing Association, Bloomington, Ind., 1966.
9. HEMPEL, DONALD J. "An Experimental Study of the Effects of Information on Consumer Product Evaluations," Paper presented at Fall Meeting, American Marketing Association, Bloomington, Ind., 1966.
10. HOLLOWAY, R. J. "Cognitive Dissonance and the Consumer: A Report on an Experiment," Unpublished manuscript, Center for Experimental Studies in Business, School of Business Administration, University of Minnesota, 1965.
11. ———. "Experimenting with Warnings," unpublished manuscript, Center for Experimental Studies in Business, School of Business Administration, University of Minnesota, 1965.
12. ———, and WHITE, TODD. "Advancing the Experimental Method in Marketing," *Journal of Marketing Research*, Vol. 1 (February, 1964), pp. 25–29.

13. HYMAN, H. H. *Interviewing in Social Research* (Chicago: University of Chicago Press), 1954.

14. KINTZ, B. L., *et al.* "The Experimenter Effect," *Psychological Bulletin*, Vol. 63 (April, 1965), pp. 223–243.

15. LINDZEY, GARDNER. "A Note on Interviewer Bias," *Journal of Applied Psychology*, Vol. 35 (June, 1951), pp. 182–184.

16. McGUIGAN, F. J. "The Experimenter: A Neglected Stimulus Object," *Psychological Bulletin*, Vol. 60 (July, 1963), pp. 421–428.

17. MITTELSTAEDT, ROBERT. "An Experimental Study of the Effects of Experience on Consumer Decision Making," Paper presented at Fall Meeting, American Marketing Association, Bloomington, Ind., 1966.

18. ORNE, M. T. "On the Social Psychology of the Psychological Experiment," *American Psychologist*, Vol. 17 (November, 1962), pp. 776–783.

19. RIECKEN, H. W. "A Program for Research on Experiments in Social Psychology," in N. F. Washburne, *Decisions, Values, and Groups*. Vol. 2 (New York: Pergamon Press), 1962, pp. 25–41.

20. ROSENTHAL, ROBERT. "Note on the Fallible E," *Psychological Reports*, Vol. 4 (December, 1958), p. 662.

21. ———. "On the Social Psychology of the Psychological Experiment: The Experimenter's Hypothesis as Unintended Determinant of Experimental Results," *American Scientist*, Vol. 51 (June, 1963), pp. 268–283.

22. ———. "Experimenter Modeling Effects as Determinants of Subjects' Responses," *Journal of Projective Techniques and Personality Assessment*, Vol. 27 (December, 1963), pp. 467–471.

23. ———. "Experimenter Outcome-orientation and the Results of the Psychological Experiment," *Psychological Bulletin*, Vol. 61 (June, 1964), pp. 405–412.

24. ———. "Letter to the Editor," *Behavioral Science*, Vol. 9 (July, 1964), pp. 256–257.

25. ———, and FODE, K. L. "Psychology of the Scientist: V. Three Experiments in Experimenter Bias," *Psychological Reports*, Vol. 12 (April, 1963), pp. 491–511.

26. ———, *et al.* "The Effect of Early Data Returns on Data Subsequently Obtained by Outcome-biased Experimenters," *Sociometry*, Vol. 26 (December, 1963), pp. 487–498.

27. ROSENTHAL, ROBERT, *et al.* "The Role of the Research Assistant in the Mediation of Experimenter Bias," *Journal of Personality*, Vol. 31 (September, 1963), pp. 313–335.

28. ROSENTHAL, ROBERT, and JACOBSON, L. "Teachers' Expectancies: Determinants of Pupils' I.Q. Gains," *Psychological Reports*, Vol. 19 (August, 1966), pp. 115–118.

29. ROSENTHAL, ROBERT, *et al.* "Variables Affecting E Bias in a Group Situation," *Genetic Psychology Monographs*, Vol. 70 (June, 1964), pp. 271–296.

30. ROSENTHAL, ROBERT, *et al.* "Instruction-Reading Behavior of the Experimenter as an Unintended Determinant of Experimental Results," *Journal of Experimental Research in Personality*, Vol. 1 (May, 1966), pp. 221–226.

31. STOERZINGER, C. A., *The Selectivity of Information After a Consumer Decision*, Unpublished master's thesis, School of Business Administration, University of Minnesota, July, 1965.

32. VENKATESAN, M. "Experimental Study of Consumer Behavior: Conformity and Independence," *Journal of Marketing Research*, Vol. 3 (November, 1966), pp. 384–387.

33. WESTLEY, BRUCE H. "Scientific Method and Communication Research," in R. O. Nafziger and D. M. White, eds., *Introduction to Mass Communication Research* (Baton Rouge: Louisiana State University Press), 1963, pp. 238–276.

Appendix D: Ethics in experimental research

Human use of human subjects: the problem of deception in social psychological experiments[1]

In 1954, in the pages of the *American Psychologist*, Edgar Vinacke raised a series of questions about experiments—particularly in the area of small groups—in which "the psychologist conceals the true purpose and conditions of the experiment, or positively misinforms the subjects, or exposes them to painful, embarrassing, or worse, experiences, without the subject's knowledge of what is going on." He summed up his concerns by asking, "What . . . is the proper balance between the interests of science and the thoughtful treatment of the persons who, innocently, supply the data?" Little effort has been made in the intervening years to seek answers to the questions he raised. During these same years, however, the problem of deception in social psychological experiments has taken on increasingly serious proportions.

The problem is actually broader, extending beyond the walls of the laboratory. It arises, for example, in various field studies in which investigators enroll as members of a group that has special interest for them so that they can observe its operations from the inside. The pervasiveness of the problem becomes even more apparent when we consider that deception is built into most of our measurement devices, since it is important to keep the respondent unaware of the personality or attitude dimension that we wish to explore. For the present purposes, however, primarily the problem of deception in the context of the social psychological experiment will be discussed.

1. Herbert C. Kelman, "Human Use of Human Subjects: The Problem of Deception in Social Psychological Experiments," *Psychological Bulletin*, Vol. 67 (January, 1967), pp. 1–11. Copyright 1967 by the American Psychological Association, and reproduced by permission.

The use of deception has become more and more extensive, and it is now a commonplace and almost standard feature of social psychological experiments. Deception has been turned into a game, often played with great skill and virtuosity. A considerable amount of the creativity and ingenuity of social psychologists is invested in the development of increasingly elaborate deception situations. Within a single experiment, deception may be built upon deception in a delicately complex structure. The literature now contains a fair number of studies in which second- or even third-order deception was employed. . . .

I hope it is clear from these remarks [omitted here: eds.] that my purpose in focusing on this problem is not to single out specific studies performed by some of my colleagues and to point a finger at them. Indeed, the finger points at me as well. I too have used deception, and have known the joys of applying my skills and ingenuity to the creation of elaborate experimental situations that the subjects would not be able to decode. I am now making active attempts to find alternatives to deception, but still I have not forsworn the use of deception under any and all circumstances. The questions I am raising, then, are addressed to myself as well as to my colleagues. They are questions with which all of us who are committed to social psychology must come to grips, lest we leave their resolution to others who have no understanding of what we are trying to accomplish.

What concerns me most is not so much that deception is used, but precisely that it is used without question. It has now become standard operating procedure in the social psychologist's laboratory. I sometimes feel that we are training a generation of students who do not know that there is any other way of doing experiments in our field— who feel that deception is as much de rigueur as significance at the .05 level. Too often deception is used not as a last resort, but as a matter of course.

Our attitude seems to be that if you can deceive, why tell the truth? It is this unquestioning acceptance, this routinization of deception, that really concerns me.

I would like to turn now to a review of the bases for my concern with the problem of deception, and then suggest some possible approaches for dealing with it.

Implications of the use of deception in social pscyhological experiments

My concern about the use of deception is based on three considerations: the ethical implications of such procedures, their methodological implications, and their implications for the future of social psychology.

1. *Ethical implications.* Ethical problems of a rather obvious nature arise in the experiments in which deception has potentially harmful consequences for the subject. Take, for example, the brilliant experiment by Mulder and Stemerding (1963) on the effects of threat on attraction to the group and need for strong leadership. In this study—one of the very rare examples of an experiment conducted in a natural setting—independent food merchants in a number of Dutch towns were brought together for group meetings, in the course of which they were informed that a large organization was planning to open up a series of supermarkets in the Netherlands. In the High Threat condition, subjects were told that there was a high probability that their town would be selected as a site for such markets, and that the advent of these markets would cause a considerable drop in their business. On the advice of the executives of the shopkeepers' organizations, who had helped to arrange the group meetings, the investigators did not reveal the experimental manipulations to their subjects. I have been worried about these Dutch merchants ever since I heard about this study for the first time. Did some of them go out of business in anticipation of the heavy competition? Do some of them have an anxiety reaction every time they see a bulldozer? Chances are that they soon forgot about this threat (unless, of course, supermarkets actually did move into town) and that it became just one of the many little moments of anxiety that must occur in every shopkeeper's life. Do we have a right, however, to add to life's little anxieties and to risk the possibility of more extensive anxiety purely for the purposes of our experiments, particularly since deception deprives the subject of the opportunity to choose whether or not he wishes to expose himself to the risks that might be entailed? . . .

But do we, for the purpose of experimentation,

have the right to provide such potentially disturbing insights to subjects who do not know that this is what they are coming for? A similar question can be raised about the Asch (1951) experiments on group pressure, although the stressfulness of the situation and the implications for the person's self concept were less intense in that context.

While the present paper is specifically focused on social psychological experiments, the problem of deception and its possibly harmful effects arises in other areas of psychological experimentation as well. . . .

So far, I have been speaking of experiments in which deception has potentially harmful consequences. I am equally concerned, however, about the less obvious cases, in which there is little danger of harmful effects, at least in the conventional sense of the term. Serious ethical issues are raised by deception per se and the kind of use of human beings that it implies. In our other interhuman relationships, most of us would never think of doing the kinds of things that we do to our subjects—exposing others to lies and tricks, deliberately misleading them about the purposes of the interaction or withholding pertinent information, making promises or giving assurances that we intend to disregard. We would view such behavior as a violation of the respect to which all fellow humans are entitled and of the whole basis of our relationship with them. Yet we seem to forget that the experimenter-subject relationship—whatever else it is—is a *real* interhuman relationship, in which we have responsibility toward the subject as another human being whose dignity we must preserve. . . .

2. *Methodological implications.* A second source of my concern about the use of deception is my increasing doubt about its adequacy as a methodology for social psychology.

A basic assumption in the use of deception is that a subject's awareness of the conditions that we are trying to create and of the phenomena that we wish to study would affect his behavior in such a way that we could not draw valid conclusions from it. For example, if we are interested in studying the effects of failure on conformity, we must create a situation in which the subjects actually feel that they have failed, and in which they can be kept unaware of our interest in observing conformity. In short, it is important to keep our subjects naive about the purposes of the experiment so that they can respond to the experimental inductions spontaneously. . . .

Since the assumptions that the subject is naive and that he sees the situation as the experimenter wishes him to see it are unwarranted, the use of deception no longer has any special obvious advantages over other experimental approaches. I am not suggesting that there may not be occasions when deception may still be the most effective procedure to use from a methodological point of view. But since it raises at least as many methodological problems as any other type of procedure does, we have every reason to explore alternative approaches and to extend our methodological inquiries to the question of the effects of using deception.

3. *Implications for the future of social psychology.* My third concern about the use of deception is based on its long-run implications for our discipline and combines both the ethical and methodological considerations that I have already raised. There is something disturbing about the idea of relying on massive deception as the basis for developing a field of inquiry. Can one really build a discipline on a foundation of such research?

From a long-range point of view, there is obviously something self-defeating about the use of deception. As we continue to carry out research of this kind, our potential subjects become more and more sophisticated, and we become less and less able to meet the conditions that our experimental procedures require. Moreover, as we continue to carry out research of this kind, our potential subjects become increasingly distrustful of us, and our future relations with them are likely to be undermined. Thus, we are confronted with the anomalous circumstance that the more research we do, the more difficult and questionable it becomes.

The use of deception also involves a contradiction between our experimental procedures and our long-range aims as scientists and teachers. In order to be able to carry out our experiments, we are concerned with maintaining the naivete of the population from which we hope to draw our subjects. . . .

. . . This perfectly understandable desire to keep procedures secret goes counter to the traditional desire of the scientist and teacher to inform and enlighten the public. To be sure, experimenters are interested only in temporary secrecy, but it is not inconceivable that at some time in the future they might be using certain procedures on a regular basis with large segments of the population and thus prefer to keep the public permanently naive. It is perhaps not too fanciful to imagine, for the long run, the possible emergence of a special class in possession of secret knowledge—a possibility that is clearly antagonistic to the principle of open communication to which we, as scientists and intellectuals, are so fervently committed.

Dealing with the problem of deception in social psychological experiments

If my concerns about the use of deception are justified, what are some of the ways in which we, as experimental social psychologists, can deal with them? I would like to suggest three steps that we can take: increase our active awareness of the problem, explore ways of counteracting and minimizing the negative effects of deception, and give careful attention to the development of new experimental techniques that dispense with the use of deception.

Some thoughts on ethics of research: after reading Milgram's "Behavioral study of obedience"[2]

Certain problems in psychological research require the experimenter to balance his career and scientific interests against the interest of his prospective subjects. When such occasions arise the experimenter's stated objective frequently is to do the best possible job with the least possible harm to his subjects. The experimenter seldom perceives in more positive terms an indebtedness to the subject for his services, perhaps because the detachment which his functions require prevents appreciation of the subject as an individual.

Yet a debt does exist, even when the subject's reason for volunteering includes course credit or monetary gain. Often a subject participates unwillingly in order to satisfy a course requirement. These requirements are of questionable merit ethically, and do not alter the experimenter's responsibility to the subject.

Most experimental conditions do not cause the subjects pain or indignity, and are sufficiently interesting or challenging to present no problem of an ethical nature to the experimenter. But where the experimental conditions expose the subject to loss of dignity, or offer him nothing of value, then the experimenter is obliged to consider the reasons why the subject volunteered and to reward him accordingly. [Italics added by authors.]

The subject's public motives for volunteering include having an enjoyable or stimulating experience, acquiring knowledge, doing the experimenter a favor which may some day be reciprocated, and making a contribution to science. These motives can be taken into account rather easily by the experimenter who is willing to spend a few minutes with the subject afterwards

2. Diana Baumrind, "Some Thoughts on Ethics of Research: After Reading Milgram's 'Behavioral Study of Obedience,' " *American Psychologist*, Vol. 19 (June, 1964), p. 421. Copyright 1964 by the American Psychological Association, and reproduced by permission.

to thank him for his participation, answer his questions, reassure him that he did well, and chat with him a bit. Most volunteers also have less manifest, but equally legitimate, motives. A subject may be seeking an opportunity to have contact with, be noticed by, and perhaps confide in a person with psychological training. The dependent attitude of most subjects toward the experimenter is an artifact of the experimental situation as well as an expression of some subjects' personal need systems at the time they volunteer.

The dependent, obedient attitude assumed by most subjects in the experimental setting is appropriate to that situation. The "game" is defined by the experimenter and he makes the rules. By volunteering, the subject agrees implicitly to assume a posture of trust and obedience. While the experimental conditions leave him exposed, the subject has the right to assume that his security and self-esteem will be protected.

. . .

References

ALLISON, RALPH I., and UHL, KENNETH P. "Influence of Beer Brand Identification on Taste Perception," *Journal of Marketing Research*, Vol. I (August, 1964), pp. 36–39.

ANDERSON, LEE K., TAYLOR, JAMES R., and HOLLOWAY, ROBERT J. "The Consumer and His Alternatives: An Experimental Approach," *Journal of Marketing Research*, Vol. III (February, 1966), pp. 62–67.

APPLEBAUM, WILLIAM, and SPEARS, RICHARD F. "Controlled Experimentation in Marketing Research," *Journal of Marketing*, Vol. XIV (January, 1950), pp. 505–516.

BAKER, DONALD J., and CHARLES H. BERRY. "The Price Elasticity of Demand for Fluid Skim Milk," *Journal of Farm Economics*, Vol. XXXV (February, 1953), pp. 124–129.

BANKS, SEYMOUR. *Experimentation in Marketing* (New York: McGraw-Hill Book Company), 1965.

BECKNELL, JAMES C., Jr. "Use of Experimental Design in the Study of Media Effectiveness," *Media/Scope* (August, 1962), pp. 46–49.

BECKNELL, JAMES C., Jr. and McISAAC, ROBERT W. "Test Marketing Cookware Coated with 'Teflon,' " *Journal of Advertising Research*, Vol. 3 (September, 1963), pp. 2–8.

BLIVEN, BRUCE, Jr. "And Now a Word from Our Sponsor," *The New Yorker* (March 23, 1963), pp. 83–130.

BORING, EDWIN G. "The Nature and History of Experimental Control," *American Journal of Psychology*, Vol. 67 (December, 1954), pp. 573 and 589.

BOYD, HARPER W., and WESTFALL, RALPH. *Marketing Research: Text and Cases*, Revised Edition (Homewood, Ill.: Richard D. Irwin, Inc.), 1964.

Business Week, "Stokely Repackages Its Canned Goods Line to Match Background with Product Color" (January 25, 1964), p. 48.

CARDOZO, RICHARD N. "An Experimental Study of Customer Effort, Expectation and Satisfaction," *Journal of Marketing Research*, Vol. II (August, 1965), pp. 244–249.

CLEMENTS, WENDELL E., HENDERSON, PETER L., and ELEY, CLEVELAND P. *The Effect of Different Levels of Promotional Expenditures on Sales of Fluid Milk* (Washington, D.C.: United States Department of Agriculture, Economic Research Service, ERS–259), October, 1965.

COX, DONALD F. "The Measurement of Information Value: A Study in Consumer Decision-Making," in William S. Decker (editor), *Emerging Concepts in Marketing*. Proceedings of the 1962 Winter Conference. (Chicago, Ill.: American Marketing Association), 1962, pp. 413–421.

COX, KEITH K. *The Relationship between Shelf Space and Product Sales in Supermarkets* (Austin, Texas: Bureau of Business Research, The University of Texas), 1964.

COX, KEITH K. "The Responsiveness of Food Sales to Supermarket Shelf Space Changes," *Journal of Marketing Research*, Vol. I (May, 1964), pp. 63–67.

DONNAHOE, ALAN S. "A New Direction for Media Research" (Richmond, Virginia: *Richmond-Times Dispatch*), 1961.

DONNAHOE, ALAN S. "The Great Roe Herring Experiment" (Richmond, Virginia: *Richmond-Times Dispatch*), undated.

EASTLACK, J. O., Jr. "Consumer Flavor Preference Factors in Food Product Design," *Journal of Marketing Research*, Vol. I (February, 1964), pp. 38–42.

EDWARDS, ALLEN L., "Experiments: Their Planning and Execution," in Gardner Lindzey (editor), *Handbook of Social Psychology*, Vol. I (Reading, Mass.: Addison-Wesley Publishing Company), 1954, pp. 259–288.

FARRELL, KENETH R. "Effects of Point-of-Sale Promotional Material on Sales of Cantaloupes," *Journal of Advertising Research*, Vol. 5 (December, 1965), pp. 8–12.

GINZBURG, ELI "Customary Prices," *American Economic Review*, Vol. XXVI, No. 2 (1936), p. 296.

GOLIN, EDWIN, and LYERLY, SAMUEL B. "The Galvanic Skin Response as a Test of Advertising Impact," *Journal of Applied Psychology*, Vol. 34 (December, 1950), pp. 440–443.

GREEN, PAUL E., and TULL, DONALD S. *Research for Marketing Decisions* (Englewood Cliffs, N.J.: Prentice-Hall, Inc.), 1966.

HAVAS, NICK, VAN DRESS, MICHAEL G., LINDSTROM, HAROLD R., and KARTALOS, PAULINE, *Consumer Acceptance of Florida Oranges with and without Color Added*. Marketing Research Report No. 537. (Washington, D.C.: U.S. Department of Agriculture, Economic Research Service), May, 1962.

HEMPEL, DONALD J. "An Experimental Study of the Effects of Information on Consumer Product Evaluations," in Raymond M. Haas (editor), *Science, Technology and Marketing.* Proceedings of the 1966 Fall Conference. (Chicago, Ill.: American Marketing Association), 1966, pp. 589–597.

HENDERSON, PETER L. *Methods of Research in Marketing: Paper Number 3. Application of the Double Change-over Design to Measure Carry-over Effects of Treatments in Controlled Experiments* (Ithaca, N.Y.: Department of Agricultural Economics, Cornell University Agricultural Experiment Station, New York State College of Agriculture, Cornell University), July, 1952.

HENDERSON, PETER L., HIND, JAMES F., and BROWN, SIDNEY E. "Sales Effects of Two Campaign Themes," *Journal of Advertising Research*, Vol. 1, No. 6 (December, 1961), pp. 2–11.

HEPNER, HARRY WALKER. *Advertising: Creative Communication with Consumers*, 4th ed. (New York: McGraw-Hill Book Company), 1964.

HESS, ECKHARD H. "Attitude and Pupil Size," *Scientific American*, 212 (April, 1965), pp. 46–54.

HOLLOWAY, ROBERT J. "An Experiment on Consumer Dissonance," *Journal of Marketing*, Vol. XXXI (January, 1967), pp. 39–43.

HOLLOWAY, ROBERT J. "Experimental Work in Marketing: Current Research and New Developments," in Frank M. Bass, Charles W. King, and Edgar A. Pessemier (editors), *Applications of the Sciences in Marketing Management* (New York: John Wiley & Sons), 1968, pp. 383–430.

HOLLOWAY, ROBERT J., and WHITE, T. "Advancing the Experimental Method in Marketing," *Journal of Marketing Research*, Vol. I (January, 1964), pp. 25–29.

HOOFNAGLE, WILLIAM S. "Experimental Designs in Measuring the Effectiveness of Promotion," *Journal of Marketing Research*, Vol. II (May, 1965), pp. 154–162.

KAPLAN, ABRAHAM. *The Conduct of Inquiry* (San Francisco, Cal.: Chandler Publishing Company), 1964.

KERLINGER, FRED N. *Foundations of Behavioral Research* (New York: Holt, Rinehart and Winston, Inc.), 1966.

KRUGMAN, HERBERT E. "Some Applications of Pupil Measurement," *Journal of Marketing Research*, Vol. I (November, 1964), pp. 15–19.

LINDSLEY, OGDEN R. "A Behavioral Measure of Television Viewing," *Journal of Advertising Research*, Vol. 2 (September, 1962), pp. 2–12.

LORIE, JAMES H., and ROBERTS, HARRY V. "Some Comments on Experimentation in Business Research," *Journal of Business*, Vol. XXIII (April, 1950), pp. 94–102.

McGUIGAN, F. J. *Experimental Psychology: A Methodological Approach*, 2nd ed. (Englewood Cliffs, N.J.: Prentice-Hall, Inc.), 1968.

McKENNA, MARY L. "The Influence of In-Store Advertising," in J. Newman (editor), *On Knowing the Consumer* (New York: John Wiley & Sons), 1966, pp. 114–115.

MARTILLA, JOHN A., and THOMPSON, DONALD L. "The Perceived Effects of 'Piggyback' Television Commercials," *Journal of Marketing Research*, Vol. III (November, 1966), pp. 365–371.

NAYLOR, JAMES C. "Deceptive Packaging: Are the Deceivers Being Deceived?" *Journal of Applied Psychology*, Vol. 46 (1962), pp. 393–398.

PAYNE, DONALD, "Looking Without Learning: Eye Movements When Viewing Print Advertisements," in M. S. Moyer and R. S. Vosburgh (editors), *Marketing For Tomorrow . . . Today.* Proceedings of the 1967 June Conference. (Chicago, Ill.: American Marketing Association), 1967, pp. 78–81.

PESSEMIER, EDGAR A. "A New Way to Determine Buying Decisions," *Journal of Marketing*, Vol. XXIV (October, 1959), pp. 41–46

RIGBY, PAUL H. *Conceptual Foundations of Business Research* (New York: John Wiley & Sons, Inc.), 1965.

ROBINSON, EDWARD J. "How an Advertisement's Size Affects Responses to It," *Journal of Advertising Research*, Vol. 3 (December, 1963), pp. 16–24.

Tide, "Shopping Cart Displays Soar Sales" (March 3, 1950), pp. 37–38.

UHL, KENNETH P. "Field Experimentation: Some Problems, Pitfalls, and Perspective," in Raymond M. Haas (editor), *Science, Technology and Marketing.* Proceedings of the 1966 Fall Conference. (Chicago, Ill. American Marketing Association), 1966, pp. 561–572.

VENKATESAN, M. "Experimental Study of Consumer Behavior: Conformity and Independence," *Journal of Marketing Research*, Vol. III (November, 1966), pp. 384–387.

VENKATESAN, M. "Laboratory Methods in Marketing Research," in M. Venkatesan and Robert Mittelstaedt (editors), *Perspectives in Marketing Research* (New York: Free Press, Inc.,) in press.

WALLERSTEIN, E. "Measuring Commercials on CATV," *Journal of Advertising Research,* Vol. 7 (June, 1967), pp. 15–19.

WEICK, K. E. "Laboratory Experimentation with Organizations," in J. G. March (editor), *Handbook of Organizations* (Chicago, Ill.: Rand McNally), 1965, pp. 194–260.

WILSON, E. BRIGHT, Jr. *An Introduction to Scientific Research* (New York: McGraw-Hill Book Company), 1952.

WOOD, A. J. "An Experimental Game," *Wood Chips,* Vol. 4 (November, 1959),pp. 1–8

9 781416 578680